The

BIG

BLACK BOOK

of

VERY DIRTY

WORDS

The
BIG
BLACK BOOK
of  DIRTY
WORDS

ALEXIS MUNIER

Aadamsmedia
Avon, Massachusetts

Published by
Adams Media, a division of F+W Media, Inc.
57 Littlefield Street, Avon, MA 02322. U.S.A.
www.adamsmedia.com

ISBN 10: 1-4405-0625-6
ISBN 13: 978-1-4405-0625-3
eISBN 10: 1-4405-0960-3
eISBN 13: 978-1-4405-0960-5

Printed in the United States of America.

10 9 8 7 6 5 4 3 2 1

Library of Congress Cataloging-in-Publication Data
is available from the publisher.

This publication is designed to provide accurate and authoritative information
with regard to the subject matter covered. It is sold with the understanding
that the publisher is not engaged in rendering legal, accounting, or other professional advice. If legal advice or other expert assistance is required, the
services of a competent professional person should be sought.
—From a *Declaration of Principles* jointly adopted by a Committee of the
American Bar Association and a Committee of Publishers and Associations

Many of the designations used by manufacturers and sellers to distinguish
their product are claimed as trademarks. Where those designations appear in
this book and Adams Media was aware of a trademark claim, the designations
have been printed with initial capital letters.

This book is available at quantity discounts for bulk purchases.
For information, please call 1-800-289-0963.

To filthy motherfuckers everywhere.

INTRODUCTION

Welcome to *The Big Black Book of Very Dirty Words*, your golden ticket to the world of *golden showers*, your answer to *answering the big question*. It's the start of a deliciously filthy journey into the netherworlds (and nether regions) of true American, British, Australian, and other sorts of forbidden English. After thorough reading, you'll delight in *brainfucking* your friends and enemies, offending your colleagues, and *pissing off* your neighbors.

In this compilation of the best sexual, dirty, and just plain old inappropriate slang English has to offer—from *giraffe* to *pudding pops*— you'll delve deeply into subject areas ripe with delectable dirty words. Each of these entries contains a definition and sample sentence so you can avoid any embarrassment while attempting to embarrass others. What's more, you'll find quotes taken from classic new films like *Superbad* and just about every movie Will Ferrell has ever made to accompany you during your *ride on the skin bus to tuna town*.

Oozing inappropriateness, you'll beg the question: is your new boyfriend *hung like a hamster*? Does your allergic girlfriend still *pet the poodle*? How do you calm an *angry dragon*? Whether you're a *fag stag* attempting to dazzle your new *pink posse* with homosexual slang or just a *banana hammock*-wearing Borat fan in search of *ricockulous* pick-up lines, *The Big Black Book of Very Dirty Words* is sure to leave you *dripping for it*. After all, language is constantly evolving—so should your potty mouth.

.

ACKNOWLEDGMENTS

A heartfelt thank you to contributors Matt Glazer, Gregory Bergman, Michael Paul Lee, T.S. Winn, Jason Niemann, Chris Robson, and Katherine Clinton Robson for their excellent work. Thanks as well to Emmanuel Tichelli, Georgina Bingham, Toby and Karen Ernberg, Coralee Elder, Bondy, Si, Jimmy, Alec, Big Gay, the Robsons, the Andersons, Derek Hambly, and David George, who all took the time to get down and dirty for this book.

$1 + 1 = 3$, n.

the sex act as procreation; *American*

> The unconventional equation, $1 + 1 = 3$, reminds us that what takes two can produce a third—a baby.

1 hole too many, adj.

someone who talks too much; *American*

> Linda has **1 hole too many**—that bitch should just shut up.

10–pin, n.

curvy woman; *American*

> As a bowling instructor, I don't get much action but still fantasize about taking home a **10-pin**.
>
> **DERIVATION:** This term is probably the most exciting bowling-derived slang in existence.

15 fingers, n.
threesome; *American*

I'm feeling like **15 fingers** this weekend.

DERIVATION: With five fingers to each hand, fifteen fingers gets you three hands, or one and a half times the fun!

16 will get you 20, n.
warning about someone's age; *American*

Dude, **16 will get you 20**—don't go there.

DERIVATION: In case you're wondering, this term reminds us of the fact that sex with someone underage will lead to a long prison sentence.

24/6, n.
always ready for a quickie except the day someone goes to church; *American*

Nicole is wet and willing **24/6**. Sunday she saves all her lovin' for the big guy in the sky.

2x4, n.
sex in four positions, hetero; *American*

Excuse the yawn, but I had to deal with a **2x4** last night.

DERIVATION: Picture two people in four positions: tittie-fucking, oral, vaginal, and anal.

39, n.
anilingus; ideograph of a person facing another's anus; *American*

After a quick **39** to moisten me up, Martin eased his throbbing cock inside my leather cheerio and the fun really began.

3-hole par, n.

sex using a woman's mouth, vagina, and anus; *American*

> That multitasker Tony made a **3-hole par**.

3 sheets to the wind, 2 sheets on the floor, n.

an easy lay; *American*

> Keep buying her drinks. **3 sheets to the wind, 2 sheets on the floor**.

> **DERIVATION:** "3 sheets to the wind" means inebriated, and thus more likely to be persuaded to have sex.

3-way, n.

a sexual threesome, usually (but not always) two women and a man; *American*

> The images of a **3-way** with the tall twins from Texas haunted his dreams for weeks.

Top Five Male Sex Fantasies

1. Sex with two women at the same time
2. Sex with two women at the same time
3. Sex with two women at the same time
4. Sex with a famous celebrity
5. Oral sex (getting it, that is)

4-11-44, n.

a powerfully large penis; *American*

> You want too much information? **4-11-44**.

> **DERIVATION:** 4 inches around times 11 inches long equals 44.

In *Dirty Harry*, Harry Callahan describes the .44 Magnum as the most powerful handgun in the world.

4:20, n.

time referring to the consumption of cannabis; *American*

Dude, it's **4:20**, roll a joint already.

Legend has it that at **4:20** every day, a group of students met up after class for a smoke. An alternative theory credits a character from one of HP Lovecraft's stories who comes out of a plant-induced hallucination to find the time is **4:20**.

4 on the floor, n.

ready to be entered from behind; *American*

Nathan likes me **4 on the floor**, but only after I've sucked him off for a good half hour.

DERIVATION: This slang comes from a car's four-speed gear box.

4-way, n.

sex that involves four people, usually (but not always) two men and two women; *American*

Think of a **4-way** as a sort of Sexual Twister game in which you play for orgasms, rather than points.

6 if you count the shadow, n.

small penis; *American*

Joe has **6 if you count the shadow**.

DERIVATION: From the penis not measuring up to average size without fudging the length.

66, n.

ideograph of male on male sex; *American*

> Route **66**? No thanks, I prefer a different sort of vacation.

69, n.

sex position in which partners give each other oral sex at the same time; *American*

> The sex position **69** is the ultimate tit for tat accommodation.

175er, n.

homosexual; pronounced 'hundred seventy fiver'; *American*

> Herr Schnabel took serious offense at the **175er** that lived next door to him.

69 Is the Loveliest Number

Called The Crow in the Kama Sutra, **69** is a nestling of bodies that allows lovers to perform oral sex on one another simultaneously—a pretty picture that has been immortalized in countless images over the ages. One such notorious engraving allegedly created by the acclaimed Belgian painter Felicien Rops in 1865 appeared in *Le Diable au Corps*—and was promptly banned *in France*. Imagine what they would have thought in Boston!

Zeig Heil

If you are a history buff, you may refer to a gay person as a **175er**.

The term dates back to 1872 and refers to § 175 of the German book of law, which forbade homosexuality. This clause was finally abolished in the 1990s after the reunification of Germany, but the slang term is used to this day, both in Germany and in English–speaking countries.

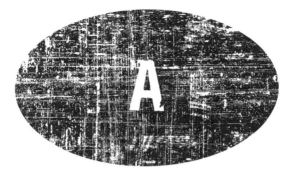

ablutophiliac, n.
sexually excited by baths or showers; *American*

> I thought my old girlfriend spent a lot of time in the bathroom. Alicia's an **ablutophiliac**.

academic bulemia, n.
the act of studying or remembering facts really quickly without learning the meaning so this knowledge can be regurgitated on an exam or test, but not retained after that exam or test; *American*

> I used **academic bulemia** to get by in college so I could concentrate on the true meaning of college: sex, drugs, and awful mistakes.

AC/DC, adj.
bisexual; *American*

> The lead singer of that popular 80s band might have jumped around on stage in pink spandex with his long hair flying about, wearing makeup, but that was just the typical glam rock of the time. And knowing all the gorgeous female groupies that adored him, I really don't think he's **AC/DC**.

acorn, n.

penis head; *American*

> If my girlfriend can't even get my **acorn** in her mouth without gagging, how am I supposed to bust a nut in there?

acrotomophilia, n.

sexual disorder involving attraction for amputees; *American*

> I thought Pete wouldn't get a lot of action when he came back from Iraq with only one leg, but thank God for the local **acrotomophilia** group.

> It's called **acrotomophilia**. But don't let them hear you call it that . . . they'll think it's a disease.
> —*Dexter*

adam, n.

ecstasy; *American*

> Conservatives like to say there was Adam and Eve, not Adam and Steve, but as long as you're high on **adam**, who really cares whose hole you stick in it?

adickted, adj.

addicted to sex or the male anatomy; *American*

> I like a good hard cock now and again but no, I wouldn't say I am **adickted**.

afterburner, n.

touching a partner's anus just before orgasm is achieved; *American*

> The astronaut's wife gave him an **afterburner** that sent him into orbit.

agate, n.
a small penis; *American*

> When it comes to family jewels, poor Phil has an **agate**.

aggro, n.
aggravation, trouble; *British*

> The missus gave me some **aggro** after I said her sister was looking sexy.

> My wife gave me some **trouble** after I said her sister was looking sexy.

agnosexual, n.
bisexual; *American*

> Somewhere between heterosexual and homosexual, the **agnosexual** is hitting on everyone.

agonophiliac, n.
person who derives pleasure from violent behavior, fighting, or combat sports; *American*

> I don't know about you, but as an **agonophiliac** I find there's nothing sexier than two chicks in a catfight—the more blood that is spilled, the more I want to spill my seed.

a-hole, n.
slang term for asshole; *American*

> I called him an **a-hole** instead of an asshole, because my mother raised me to be polite.

airplane blonde, n.

a woman with dyed blond hair who still has a black "box"; *American*

> No **airplane blondes** for me—I prefer a shaved pussy smooth.

airy-fairy, adj.

forgetful; absent-minded; *Irish*

> Colleen is just another beautiful, **airy-fairy** blonde.

> Colleen is just another beautiful, **absent-minded** blonde.

alarm clock, n.

someone who wakes you for sex; *American*

> Damn right I'm exhausted; I was woken by the **alarm clock** at 3 A.M.

aled up, adj.

drunk; *British*

> Robert was so **aled up**, he puked up in his mum's fake fire.

> Robert was so **drunk**, he threw up in his mom's fake fireplace.

algoglania, n.

sexual disorder in which pleasure is derived from pain; *American*

> My favorite **algoglania** specialist dominatrix is really a gem; the harder she spanks, the harder I wank.

alkie, n.

a wino; *British*

> That Claire, she's such a closet **alkie**. She drinks wine for breakfast.

> That Claire, she's such a closet **wino**. She has wine for breakfast.

all that and a bag of chips, adj.
awesome; *American*

> You make $7.25 an hour at Taco Bell and still think you're **all that and a bag of chips**, huh?

allergic to facial hair, n.
a woman who prefers women; lesbian; *American*

> It's clear Melissa is **allergic to facial hair** but her parents still think that bulldyke is growing a fine mustache only in between waxes.

A.m. R U Serious, n.
someone you can't believe you slept with; *American*

> I woke up this morning with a definite A.M. **R U Serious**.

ambisextrous, n.
bisexual; *American*

> Turns out my girlfriend was **ambisextrous**.

> **Ambisextrous** is a pun on ambidextrous, when someone has no preference toward using the right or left hand and employs them both equally.

anal beads, n.
string of plastic or silicone beads inserted in the anus and pulled out slowly during orgasm; *American*

> What's the dog chewing on? Shit, my **anal beads**!

anal sex, n.
copulation in which one partner thrusts his penis in his partner's anus; *American*

Anal sex is not an effective form of birth control, no matter what your boyfriend may tell you.

The Eyes Have It

"Penetrating the eye" is a doggy style anal sex position recommended in the Kama Sutra in which the partners sit up on their knees.

andromimetophilia, n.
sexual attraction to transsexuals or women who pose as men; *American*

Just as my dad used to tell me when I was growing up, there is nothing sexier than **andromimetophilia**—preferably a transsexual with a rock hard cock and big, beautiful tits.

angel dust, n.
illegal drug PCP; *American*

Angel dust was a big deal in the 80s before the speed scene took over California.

angel food, n.
gay slang for enlisted men in the Air Force; *American*

In his tight white dress uniform, Jorge was a slice of **angel food** I couldn't wait to eat.

Originally used as an elephant tranquilizer, PCP users can show superhuman strength when high, which, coupled with the aggressive behavior known to accompany the use of the drug, can be a dangerous thing.

angry dragon, n.
one with a mouth full of sperm who has been punched in the nose; *American*

When klutzy Kevin came in her mouth, he smacked her in the face, and she shot sperm out her nose. One **angry dragon**, she kicked that man right out of her bed.

anilingus, n.
oral sex performed on the anus; *American*

> I don't let my boyfriend get off easy—if I'm willing to try **anilingus**, he'd better be willing to try cunnilingus.

answer the big question, v.
to have sexual intercourse; *American*

> Sweetie, we have to talk. Maybe later we can **answer the big question**?

answer the bone-a-phone, v.
to masturbate; *American*

> After talking to my hot cousin last night, I had to **answer the bone-a-phone** like you wouldn't believe.

anteater, n.
lover with a talented tongue; *American*

> When I need to be satisfied, I look for an **anteater**.

apeshit, adj.
crazy; ballistic; *American*

> When the jealous zookeeper walked in on his favorite chimp fucking a new addition to the primate section, he went **apeshit**.

apples, n.
breasts; *American*

> Patricia has a nice pair of **apples,** but if you've seen her mom you know the apple doesn't fall far from the tree.

aquaphilia, n.
sexual fetish involving water or swimming; *American*

> The *Sports Illustrated Swimsuit Edition* is my favorite—I love those underwater **aquaphilia** shots.

....

arm candy, n.
attractive date or partner who is often brainless but beautiful; *American*

> I'm not looking for my soulmate—just some **arm candy** to bring to my sister's wedding will do for now.

> Our goal as women should be to discover who we are and not who we think we should be or who the world wants us to be. It's not our responsibility to be **arm candy**!
>
> —*Elisabeth Rohm*

around the world, n.
kissing and licking a partner's entire body; *American*

> We stayed home all weekend so we could both go **around the world**.

arse, n.
ass; *British*

> Candace only let her boyfriend fuck her in the **arse** when he was nice to her parents.

> Candace only let her boyfriend fuck her in the **ass** when he was nice to her parents.

> **DERIVATION:** Arse comes from the Old English *aers*, meaning tail, derived from the Proto-Germanic root *arsoz* for anus. Nothing to do with donkeys, as with the word *ass*.

> Yes, I've heard. Kills men by the hundreds. And if he were here, he'd consume the English with fireballs from his eyes, and bolts of lightning from his **arse**!
>
> —*Braveheart*

arse-bandit, adj.

homosexual; *British*

> Sebastien is not an **arse-bandit**. He's just into arsefucking.

> Sebastien is not a **homosexual**. He's just into assfucking.

....

arseface, n.

ugly person; dogface; *British*

> Hey, **arseface**, move your bloody arse.

> Hey, **dogface**, move your fucking ass.

Asiaphile, n.

a person with a sexual predilection toward Asian women or men; *American*

> All of those middle-aged American tourists who haunt the streets of Singapore day and night are complete **Asiaphiles**.

ass, n.

beast of burden; buttocks; moron; *American*

> Tom wanted to fuck his girlfriend in the **ass** and she said, "You are aware my shit comes out of there," but he really, *really* didn't care about that.

> **Ass** comes from the Old English *assa*, meaning donkey.

Top Ten Most Beautiful Asses in Hollywood

1. Jennifer Lopez
2. Denzel Washington
3. Beyoncé
4. Russell Crowe
5. Jessica Biel
6. Brad Pitt
7. Fergie
8. Usher
9. Cameron Diaz
10. Antonio Banderas

ass-kisser, n.

sycophant; someone who attempts to gain a personal advantage by flattery or favors; *American*

> In order to get in good with the boss, my colleague will do just about anything, including washing his car, the **ass-kisser**.

ass-to-ass, n.

The act of a large double-dildo being inserted into the asses of two people, with the dildo penetrating them until they are "ass-to-ass"; *American*

> After that huge orgy last night, I woke up to find that the excitement hadn't stopped and two girls were going **ass-to-ass** in the living room.

asswipe, n.

jerk; *American*

> Get your smelly balls out of my face, you **asswipe**!

ATM, n.

ass-to-mouth; the act of inserting one's penis in a sex partner's ass then sticking it in his or her mouth; *American*

> She told me she wanted to taste her own asshole so I gave her **ATM** right away.

attention whore, n.

someone, usually female, who craves attention at any and all costs; *American*

> His wife is such an **attention whore**, if she can't be the center of attention, she will ruin everyone's night.

attractive by default, adj.

when a person's attractiveness is influenced by his or her surroundings, the lighting, etc.; *American*

> Two beers later in the glow of the firelight, Heather was **attractive by default**.

auger, n.

penis; *American*

> I hoped Brian was going to drill me with that **auger**.

auntie, n.

older, gentle gay man; *American*

> A dick's a dick as far as I'm concerned. Be it with an **auntie**, twink, or cabana boy, I'm up for a good time.

> *Auntie Vida's gonna make you a big ol' queen, don't you worry.*
> *—To Wong Foo Thanks for Everything, Julie Newmar*

autassassinophilia, n.

sexual disorder involving pleasure derived from putting oneself in a mortally dangerous situation; *American*

> **Autassassinophilia**? Never heard of it—I just know when I stand too close to the edge of the subway platform I cream my panties.

autoerotic asphyxia, n.

when lack of oxygen leads to sexual fulfillment; *American*

> Gary is into **autoerotic asphyxia** and has been dumped by more than one girl when he has made a request for her help.

autogynephilia, n.
sexual disorder involving a man's arousal by the thought of himself as a woman; *American*

Autogynephilia is often the basis for cross-dressing.

automatic home run, n.
guaranteed sex; *American*

Sam walked over to the bar and scored an **automatic home run**.

auxter, n.
armpit; *Irish, Scottish*

Hey mate, put on some deodorant. Your **auxters** smell like shite.

Hey dude, put on some deodorant. Your **armpits** smell like shit.

avisodomy, n.
sexual fetish involving birds; *American*

Keep your parakeets away from the neighbor—we think he's into **avisodomy**.

AVN, n.

Adult Video News, the trade journal of the American adult video industry; *American*.

> My grandpa is a lifetime subscriber to **AVN**; when he bites the dust, I hope I inherit his subscription.

axed, v.

to be fired; *American*

> For just one little blow job in return, Kristen's boss assured her that when layoffs came she wouldn't be **axed**.

Aztec two-step, n.

tourista; *American*

> Mikey had planned to get laid every day during his spring break trip to Cancun, but he spent the entire week doing the **Aztec two-step** instead.

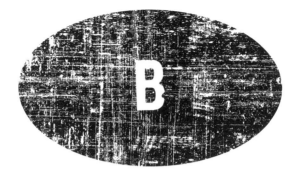

B-3, n.

behind, below, and be happy; *American*

> I think I'm going to order a **B-3** tonight.

babaloos, n.

breasts; *American*

> Forget Cheerios, I'm all about drowning your **babaloos** in my man-milk for breakfast.

babe, n.

attractive person; *American*

> My grandpa used to drive his baby blue 1962 Lincoln convertible over to school to pick us kids up. All the teachers thought he was a total **babe**.

> There are only three ages for women in Hollywood— **Babe**, District Attorney, and Driving Miss Daisy. —*Goldie Hawn*

baboon, n.

fool; *American*

> I would never date his best friend because he's a **baboon**.

baby arm, n.

penis; *American*

> My **baby arm**? Bigger than a baby's actual arm, but not quite as soft.

baby gap, n.

vagina; *American*

> Look at that huge pregnant lady over there. Soon she'll be spreading her **baby gap** wide and popping out a live one!

baby gravy, n.

semen; *American*

> Come here and get some of this **baby gravy** while it's hot and sticky.

> The house of Godric Gryffindor has commanded the respect of the wizard world for nearly ten centuries, I will not have you in the course of a single evening besmirching that name by behaving like a babbling, bumbling band of **baboons**.
> —*Harry Potter and the Goblet of Fire*

> I'll cradle the balls, stroke the shaft, work the pipe, and swallow the **gravy**. Get it over here, buddy. Let's do this.
> —*Tropic Thunder*

babydaddy, n.

father of one's child; *American*

> See that hot guy over there in the ripped jeans and slicked back hair. That's my **babydaddy**!

babymaker
penis; *American*

I put my **babymaker** in her asshole so she could avoid getting pregnant.

back-assward, adj.
backward, fucked-up; *American*

Veronica won't date anyone that's not Mexican like she is— in this day and age that is so **back-assward**.

Those are **back-assward** ways of trying to fix the economy.
—*Sarah Palin*

back door, n.
anal sex; *American*

I shouldn't have let Wayne in through the **back door** last night. This morning I'm bleeding like a stuck pig and we're all out of toilet paper.

backfire, v.
fart; *American*

I was about to go down on him when he **backfired**.

backronym, n.
a phrase that is created so that its acronym can produce a specific word; *American*

A classic **backronym** is, "For unlawful carnal knowledge" for "fuck," which has no relation to the phrase whatsoever.

I've had it with your stupid puns and **backronyms**. Can't you just speak like a normal person?

back-room bang, n.
covert sex in public places; *American*

> She led me through a door marked Employees Only for a **back-room bang**.

backyard, n.
buttocks and anus; *American*

> I told you NIMBY—not in my **backyard**, buddy!

bacon strip, n.
vagina; *American*

> I have never understood why they call it a **bacon strip**, but yours sure does look good enough to eat.

badass, n., adj.
a person who others look up to for his or her cool demeanor and rebellious attitude; being kickass; *American*

> Hey Ripley, don't worry. Me and my squad of ultimate **badasses** will protect you.
> —*Aliens*

> Damn, Toby, look at your **badass** self with those shiny new penny loafers and navy blazer!

bad egg, n.
corrupt, untrustworthy person; *American*

> Billy's brother is a **bad egg**—he probably would sell out his own mother if he could.

> Bad bird, **bad egg**.
> —*German proverb*

bag, v., adj.

to score someone as a trophy; *American*

> I **bagged** that famous disc jockey who was at the bar.

....

bagel, n.

Jewish woman or gay Jewish man; *American*

> I had a **bagel** for breakfast. And lunch. And supper.

Bagels are one of America's favorite foods with a hole in the middle, second only to donuts. Knoshing on a bagel any time of the day or night is appropriate, or as often as you can cream the cheese.

....

bagpiping, n.

performing the sex act in a partner's armpit; *American*

> All my life, I haven't liked raising my hand in class, and now, unfortunately, I've married a man who's into **bagpiping**.

....

bagsie, v.

to call dibs; *British*

> As usual, Tom **bagsied** on that hot lady before I had even seen her.

> As usual, Tom **called dibbs** on that biddy before I had even seen her.

....

bahookie, n.

bottom; *British*

> Oi, I wouldn't mind that fit bird's **bahookie** in my face at this very moment.

> Hey, I wouldn't mind that girl's **ass** in my face at this very moment.

That was just a warning. Try it again, I'll be kicking your furry, brown **bahookie**!
—*Open Season*

balcony, n.

large breasts supported by a bra; *American*

> I like to splurge on balcony seats at the opera so I can check out the **balconies** on stage as well.

ball sack rest rack, n.

breasts; *American*

> When you're in need of a break, there's no better stress reliever than a **ball sack rest rack.**

ball-and-chain, n.

marriage; *American*

> Sheila shits bricks when Andy talks about his **ball-and-chain**.

Well, gotta run. You know how it is, the old **ball-and-chain**.
—*Chuck*

baller, n.

a popular or well-liked thug; *American*

> You can tell that **baller** to shut his cocky ass mouth or I'll do it for him.

balloon knot, n.

anus; *British*

> When she spread my bum cheeks and started licking my **balloon knot**, I almost shot my wad.

> When she spread my butt cheeks and started licking my **asshole**, I almost shot my wad.

Baltic, adj.

awesome; cool; *Irish*

> The film was **Baltic**, mate, so it was.

> Dude, the movie was **awesome**.

....

Bama, n.

hick; person from Alabama; *American*

> You can always tell a **Bama**, but you can't tell him much.

....

Bambisexual, adj.

asexual; *American*

> With his doe eyes and iffy sexual preferences, Michael Jackson, may he rest in peace, was the quintessential **Bambisexual**.

> **DERIVATION:** Bambi, the beloved deer of the Disney cartoon of the same name, shows very few overtly masculine traits, hence the meaning of this term.

....

banana hammock, n.

skimpy men's underwear; *American*

> Last summer we spent a week on Italy's beaches and the **banana hammocks** were out of control.

....

banana split, n.

shit; *British*

> Let's wait before ordering a pudding; right now, I have got to run to the toilet for a **banana split**.

> Let's wait before ordering dessert; right now, I have got to run to the bathroom to take a **shit**.

bang, v.

to have sex with; *American*

> I just wanted to **bang** her, but she wanted a relationship. So after we fucked, I asked her to marry me. She turned me down flat.
>
> **DERIVATION:** The word bang comes from the Old Norse *banga,* meaning to hammer.

bang the drums, v.

to energetically fuck someone from behind; *American*

> I fantasized about **banging the drums** with my high school band leader until his ass was dripping red.

bang the shit out of her, v.

to have a long bout of energetic sex; *American*

> Bang her? I **banged the shit out of her**.

You know, that's such a lovely image—"fuck her brains out." It ranks right up there with that other classic: "**bang the shit out of her**."
—*City Slickers*

bang-up job, n.

well-done assignment or project despite a lack of knowledge or time; *American*

> You may be just an amateur taxidermist, but you did a real **bang-up job** on that skunk roadkill.

Oh, gee, thanks, Dave. **Bang-up job** so far. Extortion, coercion.
—*The Usual Suspects*

banjaxed, adj.

drunk; *Scottish*

> Beer or liquor, no mind. As long as I'm **banjaxed** and the missus is furious, that's all that matters.
>
> Beer or liquor, doesn't matter. As long as I'm **drunk** and my old lady is furious, that's all that matters.

bareback, n.

unprotected anal sex; *American*

> It might be dangerous, but we can all admit riding **bareback** feels so much better than using a condom.

barely legal, adj.

just above the age of consent; *American*

> I couldn't believe that young girl he's dating. She's **barely legal**.

barmy, adj.

crazy; *British*

> Your old lady's a bit **barmy**, ain't she?
>
> Your girlfriend's a little **crazy**, isn't she?

barnacles, n.

bits of toilet paper stuck on nether regions; *American*

> Nothing kills the mood like going south and finding **barnacles** down there.

barse, n.

perineum; area from balls to ass; *British*

> I got my **barse** pierced last weekend. It was a good thing I was fucking hammered at the time.
>
> I got my **perineum** pierced last weekend. It was a good thing I was fucking hammered at the time.

bash the bishop, v.

to jerk off; *British*

> John was **bashing the bishop** when his grandmother called, and continued jerking off after the call.

> John was **jerking off** when his grandmother called, and continued jerking off after the call.

basket weaver, n.

someone who adjusts their crotch in tight pants; *American*

> At the club last night there was this Native American **basket weaver** constantly repositioning his package, and judging by the size of things, he can paddle my pink canoe anytime.

bastard, n.

the literal meaning is a person who is born of parents who aren't married; derogatory term for someone you don't like; *American*

> Even if the **bastard** didn't sleep with my wife, he's still a **bastard** because, what, is my wife not good enough for him?

> You want to know who you are? Huh? Huh? You don't, I do, everyone does . . . you're the son of a thousand fathers, all **bastards** like you.
> —*The Good, the Bad, and the Ugly*

bat for both sides, adj.

to be bisexual; *American*

> Winona **bats for both sides**, so Xavier really shouldn't even try hitting on her. He'd lose out to all that competition from both sexes.

> He **hits from both sides** of the plate. He's amphibious.
> —*Yogi Berra*

bat for the other side, adj.
to be gay; *American*

> Don't get your hopes up, Alison, he **bats for the other side**.

batch, n.
single, bachelor; *British*

> I'm on the pull tonight. Is your fit cousin Eric a **batch**?

> I'm looking to score tonight. Is your hot cousin Eric a **bachelor**?

battered, adj.
destroyed; *British*

> Simon must've necked lots of E last night. He looks **battered**.

> Simon must've dropped lots of E last night. He looks **destroyed**.

BBBJ, n.
bareback blowjob; blowjob when the male isn't wearing a condom, versus CBJ, blowjob with a condom; *American*

> Even better than a PB&J is a **BBBJ**.

BD, n.
a month with two periods; *American*

> First, my car died, and now I'm having a **BD**.

> **DERIVATION:** This term comes from a baker's dozen, or thirteen. Can also be explained to eavesdroppers as "bad day."

bean queen, n.

homosexual man who prefers Hispanics; *American*

> After a few years together with his lover Carlos, we affectionately referred to George as a **bean queen**.

bear, n.

masculine, muscular, hairy, homosexual man; *American*

> Cecil usually watches football to fantasize that the players are all **bears** who want him.

> He's a **bear**, you see some gay guys are twinks and others are **bears**, this gay guy is a **bear**. By the way, we are totally cool with that, to each his own.
> —*It's Always Sunny in Philadelphia*

bear paw, v.

to scratch oneself while reaching into pants; this is usually frowned upon in most circles; *American*

> The other day, Paul and I were in a restaurant, and he actually **bear pawed** his nuts in front of everyone.

bearded clam, n.

an unkempt, hairy, and generally unattractive vagina; *American*

> When a girl gets bikini ready for Rio, she trims her **bearded clam**.

beast with two backs, n.

a couple locked in intercourse; *British*

I entered the room expecting to find my roommate but instead I saw the **beast with two backs**.

I entered the room expecting to find my roommate but instead I saw him **having sex with his girlfriend**.

I am one, sir, that comes to tell you, your daughter and the Moor are now making the **beast with two backs**.
—*Othello, Act 1, Scene 1, William Shakespeare*

beastly, adj.

nasty; *American*

Jim woke up with a hangover and a **beastly** woman sleeping next to him. He vowed never to drink tequila again.

beat the meat, v.

to jerk off; *British*

I like to **beat the meat** in the morning after a good night's sleep.

I like to **masturbate** in the morning after a good night's sleep.

beat the rug, v.

have sex; *American*

Let's skip dusting and just **beat the rug**.

DERIVATION: Beating the rug implies the act of pounding against the genital thatch.

beaver, n.

pussy; *American*

Her **beaver** was a forest in which I longed to lose myself.

Nice **beaver**!
—*The Naked Gun*

bee stings, n.
small breasts; *British*

> The French prefer **bee stings** to corking milkers.

> The French prefer **small breasts** to huge titties.

beef bayonet, n.
penis; *American*

> When at war, soldiers don't see a lot of action with their **beef bayonets**.

beef curtains, n.
a vagina whose outer labia is constantly swollen and engorged from copious amounts of intercourse; *American*

> On that first weekend together we had so much sex that my girlfriend's **beef curtains** were big enough to hide behind by the time Monday rolled around.

Belfast breakfast, n.
the act of blowing someone up or setting their genitals on fire; *Irish*

> Just porridge for me thanks, I don't have much time before my **Belfast breakfast**.

This began as an IRA torture method to English crown loyalists in the 1800s. Most often, a person's pants were drenched in alcohol and they were then lit afire.

bell end, n.
dick head; *British*

My mate once shagged a girl who vengefully attempted to bite off his **bell end** because he said her new jeans made her look fat. He obviously knew nothing about women.

My friend once fucked a girl who vengefully attempted to bite off his **dick** because he said her new jeans made her look fat. He obviously knew nothing about women.

belly jelly, n.
cum on his or her belly; *American*

My girlfriend likes to eat **belly jelly**, but I prefer the taste of Jelly Bellies.

bender, n.
queer, homo; *British*

I have no problem with his being a **bender**, except when he tries to stick his goolies in my mouth.

I have no problem with his being a **homo**, except when he tries to teabag me.

bestiality, n.
sex with an animal or animals; *American*

Hey, my dog isn't in to **bestiality**, so don't get any ideas.

Randal: You're in the **bestiality** business.
Sexy Stud: Hey fucko! We like to call it inter-species erotica.
—*Clerks II*

better 30 than 9, interj.

suggestion to use a condom; *American*

> Think again. **Better 30 than 9**.
>
> **DERIVATION:** From the length of time it might take to put on a condom (thirty seconds) versus the nine months of a pregnancy.

bevvied, adj.

drunk; *British*

> We were going to go for a couple more after the game, but I was so **bevvied** that I puked on a few of my friends and the night was over for me—and them.
>
> We were going to go for a couple more beers after the game, but I was so **drunk** that I puked on a few of my friends and the night was over for me—and them.

BFP, n.

bound for pleasure, bondage; *American*

> Sorry I'm late, but I was **BFP**.

biastophilia, n.

sexual disorder involving pleasure derived from performing the act of rape; *American*

> What kind of a sick fuck gets off on **biastophilia**? They deserve to be raped themselves, preferably during a long prison sentence.

bi-curious, adj.

not bisexual, but willing to think about it; *American*

> My ex was straight, but **bi-curious**.

biddy, n.

a cute girl; *American*

> I want to tap that **biddy** with the smoking ass.
>
> **DERIVATION:** Biddy is a surprisingly flattering derivation of the derogatory word bitch.

> Oh, great, an 80-year-old, grouchy, pretentious, smoking hot **biddy**!
> —*Scrubs*

biff, n.

vagina; *British*

> I think the bird who sits opposite me in math is well up for it—she's always flashing me her **biff**.

> I think the chick who sits across from me in math class wants my dick badly—she's always flashing me her **pussy**.

big enchilada, n.

penis; *American*

> Carlos may have been pint-sized, but my God, you should've seen the size of his **big enchilada**.

big event, n.

sex; *American*

> Get ready for the **big event** . . . you know it only happens a few times a year.

to big-note oneself, v.

to brag; *Australian*

> I don't mean to **big-note myself**, but I beat out four other trombonists for the Mozart solo.

> I don't mean to **brag**, but I beat out four other trombonists for the Mozart solo.

bike, n.
a slut; *American*

> My sister was the dorm **bike** her freshman year at ASU.

the bill, n.
the man, the police; *British*

> I was pulled over by **the bill** last night for speeding and fuzzy dice.

> I got stopped by **the police** last night for speeding and fuzzy dice.

bimbo, n.
a stupid woman or man; *American*

> He got that **bimbo** to go home with him because he proved to her he was a doctor by showing her his toy stethoscope.

> . . . I'm not gonna parade around in a swimsuit like some airhead **bimbo** that goes by the name Gracie Lou Freebush and all she wants is world peace. . . .
> —*Miss Congeniality*

bingo wings, n.
flabby upper arms; *British*

> Look at the **bingo wings** on Grandma!

> Look at the **flabby arms** on Grandma!

binoculars, n.
a pair of breasts worth examining; *American*

> Watch out, **binoculars** coming up on your left.

birdbrain, n.
stupid man or woman; *American*

> I bet even Steven could score with that **birdbrain** over there.

They're already making a movie about Paris Hilton being in jail. I believe they're calling it *The Bird Brain* of *Alcatraz*.
—*David Letterman*

bisecting the triangle, n.
heterosexual sexual intercourse; *American*

> And for my homework tonight, I think I'm going to **bisect a triangle**.

> **DERIVATION:** The term triangle refers to the vagina.

bishop, n.
penis; *American*

> Wait until after confession and I'll introduce you to the **bishop**.

a bit of crumpet, n.
a woman who is good enough to eat (sexual sense); *British*

> Tess is **a bit of crumpet**, and I would start with her arse.

> Tess is **the kind of girl I would eat out**, and I would start with her ass.

a bit on the side, n.
affair; *American*

> She knew he had **a bit on the side** when she came home early and found him screwing her Pilates instructor.

bitch, n.

A whiny woman or man; a person who is whipped into doing whatever his or her partner tells him or her to do; *American*

> He's such a little **bitch** that when his girlfriend orders him to pick up her dog's shit, he actually does it.

> Sometimes you have to be a high-riding **bitch** to survive. Sometimes being a **bitch** is all a woman has to hold onto.
> —*Dolores Claiborne*

bitchslap, n.

an overwhelming, backhanded slap to someone's face; a verbal thrashing of someone out of line or off base; *American*

> My ultimate **bitchslap**? Sarah Palin, hands down.

> Someday, you gonna get **bitchslapped** and I'm not gonna do a thing to stop it.
> —*10 Things I Hate about You*

bite the pillow, v.

to receive anal sex; *American*

> Get ready to **bite the pillow**.

the bizzies, n.

the police; *British*

> **The bizzies** have a lot of work to do in Liverpool 'cause half the city are thieves.

> **The police** have a lot of work to do in Liverpool 'cause half the city are thieves.

black jack, n.
penis of color; *American*

> How's about we head to the club for a little **black jack** tonight?

black-and-white, n.
black male wearing a white condom; *American*

> I went to the party looking for a **black-and-white** and came home with a handsome oreo.

black-bag operation, n.
a covert meeting; a lover whose identity must be concealed; *American*

> I don't talk about my boyfriend because he's a **black-bag operation**.

blackberry, n.
vagina of color; *American*

> You know what they say—the darker the **blackberry**, the sweeter the juice.

bladdered, adj.
drunk, wasted; *British*

> The groomsmen were completely **bladdered** on the wedding day after a wild night of debauchery that would make Hunter S. Thompson proud.

> The groomsmen were completely **wasted** on the wedding day after a wild night of debauchery that would make Hunter S. Thompson proud.

blamestorming, v.

group decision-making on who is to blame; *American*

> If no one confesses to breaking the copy machine soon, the **blamestorming** session will continue all day.

blast, n.

mouthful of smoke; *British*

> Stop bogarting that roach and give me a **blast** of it.

> Stop bogarting that roach and let me get a **mouthful of smoke**.

blaze, v.

to smoke marijuana; *British*

> Let's skive chemistry and **blaze** up behind the bike shed.

> Let's cut chemistry and **smoke** some weed behind the bike shed.

blazes, adj.

very attractive; *American*

> Even as her age approaches her IQ, Madonna is so hot, she's **blazes**.

bleed, n.

menstruating; *American*

> I'm so horny I might pretend not to notice my girlfriend is on the **bleed**.

bleep, n.
fuck; *American*

> Let's **bleep** and get it over with.

> **DERIVATION:** This term comes from censors bleeping over offensive words.

The Worst Substitute Swears
1. Fudge
2. H, E, double toothpicks
3. Gosh darn it
4. Cow patties
5. Aw shucks

blind, adj.
uncircumsized; *American*

> Careful—that guy with the stick and the dark sunglasses is Italian, and therefore, probably **blind**.

blinding, adj.
fantastic; *British*

> I went to see Radiohead last night. They were fucking **blinding**.

> I went to see Radiohead last night. They were fucking **fantastic**.

blondorexia, n.
the overwhelming desire to become ever blonder; *American*

> Long, dark locks may have been trendy in Cindy Crawford's days, but now it's stars with **blondorexia** like Pink and Paris Hilton that make the tabloids.

bloody, adj.
damn; *British*

Get your **bloody** hands off me!

Get your **damn** hands off me!

DERIVATION: The word bloody is a very offensive term in England, where its derivation is still being debated. Some say it comes from a derogatory form of "blueblood," used by commoners to put down aristocrats. Others insist that it refers to menstrual blood. Another theory is that the term is a sacrilegious variation of "God's Blood" or "By Our Lady."

Life is to be lived. If you have to support yourself, you had **bloody** well better find some way that is going to be interesting. And you don't do that by sitting around.
—*Katharine Hepburn*

bloody vaginal belch, n.
a rarely seen phenomenon in which a woman on her period expels air from her vagina with enough force to be likened to a wet burp; *American*

We were in bed, and she let loose a **bloody vaginal belch** that may have been the most hellacious sound ever heard.

blouse, v.
when a woman undoes enough buttons to expose her breasts; *American*

While I pumped gas, the girl at the pump to my right **bloused** me.

blow a load, v.
to ejaculate; *American*

When I **blew my load** on her face and didn't warn her, she kicked me in the balls.

blow chunks, v.

to vomit; *American*

> Drink as much as you want, but **blow chunks** on my new carpet and you'll never be invited back.

blowie, n.

cutesy term for oral sex performed on a man; *American*

> Aw, sweetie, sorry you had such a rough day at work. Would a wittle-bittie **blowie** make you feel better?

blowjob, n.

a sexual act where a man receives oral sex; *American*

> She was so drunk last night that when she gave him a **blowjob** at the party, she volunteered to swallow.

blow-up doll, n.

a woman good for nothing but sex; *American*

> Katie? She's just a **blow-up doll**.

blue balls, n.

soreness of the scrotum caused from a long period without an orgasm; *American*

> My wife has been holding out on sex for weeks; my **blue balls** may never go away.

blue shade of pink, n.
lesbian; *American*

Jonathon's sister is a **blue shade of pink**.

DERIVATIVE: Blue is for boys, pink is for girls, hence the slightly masculine female implied by this expression.

---

blumpkin, n.
a sexual act where a man receives a blowjob while taking a shit; *American*

She was so shit-faced I got her to give me a **blumpkin**. Then she threw up in my lap.

Bobbitt, v.
to cut off someone's penis; *American*

I'm so mad at Herb for sleeping with my mom that I could **Bobbitt** him.

John Bobbitt was the inspiration for this slang term. After his wife Lorena cut off his dick and threw it out her car window, he made a few pornos before settling down to work in construction.

---

bodacious, adj.
very attractive person; *American*

That woman in the library was so **bodacious** that I skipped my usual dirty talk with the librarian.

Look at them **bodacious** set of ta-tas.
—*An Officer and a Gentleman*

---

boff, v.
to fart; *British*

Brussels sprouts make me **boff**.

Brussels sprouts make me **fart**.

DERIVATION: Boff can also mean to have sex, so maybe brussels sprouts put you in the mood for that too.

I thought **Boff** was the name of a locale . . . you know, the name of a district.
—*Fawlty Towers*

bog standard, adj.
ordinary; plain; *Australian*

> I'd take a **bog standard** Sheila over a sexy lass any day—less risk of her cheating on a mug–faced bloke like me.

> I'd take a **plain** Jane over a hottie any day—less risk of her cheating on a dog like me.

bogging, adj.
disgusting, smelly; *Scottish*

> Get your **bogging** bollocks out of my face!

> Get your **smelly** balls out of my face!

boiler, n.
dog; *British*

> Ask Prudence out? Not a chance; she hit every branch of the ugly tree on the way down. She's a proper **boiler**.

> Ask Prudence out? Not a chance; she was hit with the ugly stick. She's a real **dog**.

bollock someone, v.
to tell someone off; *British*

> My boyfriend **bollocked me** for staying out all night.

> My boyfriend **told me off** for staying out all night.

bollocks, n.

bullshit; lit. testicles; *British*

Bollocks! There's no way she'll let you have sex with her after you forgot to feed her cat while she was away.

Bullshit! There's no way she'll let you have sex with her after you forgot to feed her cat while she was away.

DERIVATION: The Anglo-Saxon word bollocks meaning testicles comes from the Teutonic word ball, meaning "to swell." By the seventeenth century, it was also used to describe priests delivering silly sermons—hence its current usage for "nonsense."

Never Mind the Bollocks

In 1977, the Sex Pistols produced an album titled *Never Mind the Bollocks, Here's the Sex Pistols*. The punk rockers were later taken to court on obscenity charges—but thanks to acclaimed linguistics professor James Kingsley, the charges were dismissed. Kingsley convinced the court that the word bollocks could also refer to the clergy—and to silliness itself. And the Sex Pistols are nothing if not silly.

That is total **bollocks**. You've actually gone mad, now.
—*Love Actually*

bomb diggity, n.

something or someone who is awesome and/or cool; *American*

When I told Molly she was the **bomb diggity,** she responded, "You should invent a time machine and go back in time to when it was cool to say that."

Whittier: Monica, if you want to be the **bomb diggity**, you have to act like the **bomb diggity**, and Tina is the **bomb diggity**!
Monica: Did she just say "**bomb diggity**" three times in one sentence?
—*Bring It On Again*

A **B** C D E F G H I J K L M N O P Q R S T U V W X Y Z

bone, v.
to fuck someone; *American*

> I want to **bone** that chick but I'm afraid my penis might fall off from all of her STDs.

bone smuggler, n.
drag queen; *American*

> Don't let that **bone smuggler** fool you—he's 100 percent cock.

bonehead, n.
idiot; *American*

> Listen, **bonehead**, your sandwich was $4.99. You gave me a five and I gave you back a penny, so what's your beef?

boner, n.
hard-on; *American*

> His **boner** was tremendous, but I always get this awful feeling it's like fake tits because he uses Viagra.

boob tube, n.
tube top; *British*

> No offense, but your sister shouldn't wear a **boob tube** until she loses a stone.

> No offense, but your sister shouldn't wear a **tube top** until she loses fifteen pounds.

> **DERIVATION:** "Boob tube" also means television in America, so one could say, "If she didn't spend so much time in front of the boob tube, she would be able to fit into her boob tube."

> You know, that last drill we had, I was about to finally **bone** my girlfriend, and then we heard that there was this drill, and she told me there was no way.
> —*The Family Guy*

> Just imagine if girls weren't weirded out by our **boners** and stuff, and just like wanted to see them. That's the world I one day want to live in.
> —*Superbad*

book it, v.

to leave hurriedly; *American*

> If we want to make the orgy on time, honey, we'd better **book it**.

boomerang, n.

a man who comes too quickly; *American*

> Rick is such a **boomerang** that sometimes I forget if we had sex.

boon to the birth-control industry, n.

someone who sleeps around; *American*

> That president was such a tramp—a real **boon to the birth-control industry**.

booty call, n.

a call at night with the explicit intent of having sex; *American*

> Tiffany was always good for a **booty call**, but the logistics grew more difficult after she got married.

That's what a girl wants to hear: "Darling, do all the weird crap you like, just don't be late for the **booty call**."
—*Veronica Mars*

booze-whore, n.

a slut who uses a guy to pay for her drink(s) then gives him nothing but the bill; *American*

> That **booze-whore** tried to steal my drink right out of my hand, but I pulled the shot glass away just in time to gulp the whiskey down myself.

bop the top, v.
to fuck a woman's breasts; *American*

> Though I don't mind **bopping the top** once in a while, I definitely prefer a good ass fucking.

bottle, v.
to take ownership; *American*

> I'm going to **bottle** me some of that.

> **DERIVATION:** This term comes from putting something in a bottle and calling it your own.

bottom, n.
homosexual man who prefers receiving anal sex to performing it; *American*

> Clyde put an ad in the personals for a hairy **bottom** who enjoys long walks in the park and fine wine, but hasn't had any replies yet.

box lunch, n.
cunnilingus; *American*

> I ate a **box lunch** yesterday.

Brad, n.
shit; *British*

> Pull the car over mate; I've got to take a **Brad**.

> Pull the car over dude; I've got to take a **shit**.

brain nuts, n.

this is the term for removing the cerebral cortex that controls fear and reason and replacing it with an extra set of testicles; masculinity; *American*

> Those dudes on *Jackass* have some serious **brain nuts** . . . also, they must be on *a lot* of drugs.

> **DERIVATION:** Coined by former *Daily Show* correspondent Rob Riggle during one of his segments on the show.

brainfuck, v.

to purposely confuse someone; *American*

> Did you seriously sleep with my mom or are you **brainfucking** me?

breasticles, n.

breasts; *American*

> When it's hot outside, I can feel the sweat dripping down between my **breasticles**.

breasts, n.

mammary glands of a woman; *American*

> Nothing can bring a man to his knees faster than a beautiful pair of **breasts**.

Synonyms for Breasts:

appetizers
assets
attention getters
baby feeders
bad boys
balloons
bangers
bazongas
bazookas
Berthas
biscuits
bombs
bongos
boobies
boobs
boobsters
bosom
bottle rockets
boulders
bouncers
bra stuffers
brown eyes
bubbles
bullseyes
bust
Charleys
chest
chesticles
chitty chitty bang bangs
cleavage
coconuts
desk pillows
dumplings
flapdoodles
flotation devices
Fred and Ethel
glands
globes
golden orbs
grillwork

gunzagas
hangers
head rests
headlights
heffers
high beams
hills
hogans
hood ornaments
hot dog buns
humps
itty bitty titties
Jackie Chan and Bruce Lee
jiggly puffs
jobbers
jolly jigglers
jolly jugs o' joy
kaboobers
knobs
the ladies
luscious fruits
mammaries
mammies
man pacifiers
mangos
meat puppets
melons
milk bags
milk duds
milk jugs
milk makers
milk wagons
milkers
milkshakes
moo moos
mosquito bites
mounds
mountains
muffins
nipple sporters

nodules
norks
nose warmers
the objects of my erection
pancakes
paper weights
pears
pillows
puppies
queen of the navigational beacons
rib bumpers
rib cushion
sandbags
scoops
snuggle pups
speed balls
speed bumps
sugar lumps
sweater cows
sweater kittens
sweater muppets
ta tas
teats
tee tees
Thelma and Louise
torpedoes
Tweedledum and Tweedledee
tweeters
twin peaks
the twins
udders
water balloons
watermelons
wet tea bags
who let the dogs out
Wilsons
window washers
wobblesteaks
ying-yangs

breeder, n.
person worth having children with; *American*

> Your hubby may not be able to hold down a good job, but if you take into account his good looks and personality, he's definitely a **breeder**.

Bristols, n.
tits; *British*

> Do you see that fit bird's **Bristols**? Fantastic!

> Do you see that biddy's **tits**? Fantastic!

bromance, n.
platonic love between two men; *American*

> Sometimes Shelley thinks her boyfriend and his best friend Chuck have more than a **bromance** because they finish each other's sentences. As long as that's all they finish.

> Archibald, isn't it about time you ended this **bromance**? What happens at Yale stays at Yale.
> —*Gossip Girl*

brotherfucker, n.
homosexual; *American*

> Well that's just great—I spend a fortune on a new hairdo and sexy lingerie, and it turns out you set me up with a **brotherfucker**.

brown bag, n.
condom after dirty anal sex; *American*

> There was no time for a pre-performance enema before the porn filming started, so the cameraman cleverly panned away as the **brown bag** was removed in preparation for the money shot.

brown eye, n.
anus, asshole; *American*

> George was an anal freak; as soon as she touched his **brown eye**, he cried like a baby.

> My mom says my dad has **brown eyes** because he is full of shit.
> —*Jersey Girl*

brown paper bag, n.
a woman who dresses to downplay her attractiveness; *American*

> Keisha is a **brown paper bag**. She always wears sweats but you can still make out her awesome booty if you try.

brown-eyed mullet, n.
feces in a body of water; *American*

> I took my ten-year-old nephew on a fishing trip for his birthday, but he was more interested in the **brown-eyed mullet** we found floating in the lake.

Bruce, n.
a gay man; *American*

> That guy wearing the pink flowered shirt? He's such a **Bruce**.

bubble wrap, n.
raised areas of flesh some women experience before orgasm; *American*

> I love petting Tonya's **bubble wrap**.

buff puff, n.
muscular homosexual male; *American*

> No **buff puffs** for André; he only dates computer engineers.

buffugly, adj.

extremely unattractive; *American*

> Have you seen the new Matt Damon movie? Normally he's a hottie but with those extra pounds and glasses, he's totally **buffugly**.

> **DERIVATION:** Buffugly is short for the term butt fucking ugly.

bugchasing, n.

the act of a homosexual man knowingly pursuing sexual activity with HIV-infected men; *American*

> **Bugchasing** has to be one of the stupidest fetishes—some guys have a real death wish.

bugger, v.

to have anal sex; *British*

> The bigger the biggie, the better the **bugger**.

bugger off, v.

get lost; *British*

> **Bugger off** or I'll call the police, you dirty Tyke.

> **Get lost** or I'll call the police, you dirty Yorkshireman.

bukkake, n.

multiple men ejaculating on a woman's face, usually one after the other; *American*

> When it comes to weird sexual practices like **bukkake**, no one, not even the Germans, can beat the Japanese.

bullshit, n.

nonsense or an obvious lie; *American*

> Most politicians have campaign promises that are **bullshit**, so don't expect that tax break to pay for all of your sex dolls.

> Love is **bullshit**. Emotion is **bullshit**. I am a rock. A jerk. I'm an uncaring asshole and proud of it.
> —*Chuck Palahniuk*

bum chum, n.

gay friend or lover; *British*

> Tell me that bloke in the pink sweater isn't your **bum chum**!

> Tell me that guy in the pink sweater isn't your **gay lover**!

bump uglies, v.

to have sex; *American*

> If I fail in my attempt to **bump uglies** with that pocket nymph over there, I'll probably instead just choke my chicken to Japanese porn.

> Did you **bump uglies** with my sister?
> —*Tango and Cash*

bumper cars, n.

sex; *American*

> After we got back from the carnival, Jessica was in the mood for **bumper cars**.

bumpers, n.

breasts; *American*

> Amazing how even thirteen-year-olds these days sport big **bumpers**—must be the hormones in the water.

bunghole, n.

anus; *American*

> Put on some underwear or get your smelly **bunghole** off my couch!

---

bunker shy, adj.

shy of anal sex; *American*

> You know what they say: Once **bunker shy**, twice bitten.

> **DERIVATION:** Understandably, many men are afraid to enter prison and find an over-friendly bunkmate.

> Beavis: Hey Butthead, is it normal for the inside of your **bunghole** to itch?
> Butthead: Beavis, it's not even normal to ask.
> —*Beavis and Butthead*

---

bunting, n.

settling for less than intercourse; *American*

> I'm **bunting** tonight, rather than taking the risk of rushing things.

> **DERIVATION:** From the baseball term, making a short hit to get on base rather than swinging for a homerun.

---

buppie, n.

bisexual young urban professional; *American*

> Be it for cock or pussy, **buppies** aren't afraid to show off their excellent taste.

---

burn the broccoli, v.

to smoke marijuana; *American*

> Dude, let's just skip woodshop and **burn the broccoli** instead.

burrito, n.
penis; *American*

> After two taco supremes, Kayla was in no mood for a big beef **burrito**.

bury the bone, v.
to have sex; *American*

> At midnight, I usually take our poodle out to take a dump and **bury the bone** with any neighborhood strays.

bush, n.
heroin; *British*

> My friend Wesley injects **bush** straight into the veins in his feet; he makes me feel better about myself.

> My friend Wesley injects **heroin** straight into the veins in his feet; he makes me feel better about myself.

bush, n.
hairy vagina; *American*

> The hairier the better, but the only problem with going down on a big old **bush** is getting pubic hair stuck in your teeth.

> She's got a **bush** like a porcupine!
> —*I Love You, Man*

bushwhacked, adj.
worn out from sex with a woman; *American*

> Make that coffee super large. I'm **bushwhacked**.

bust a nut, v.
to ejaculate; *American*

> She's so hot that I would **bust a nut** if she just looked at me . . . uh oh . . . did she just make eye contact?

I'm gonna **bust a nut** up in this bitch right now!
—*Grindhouse*

butch, adj.
lesbian who acts and looks like a man; *American*

> Sure, I'd go to bed with a lesbian if she weren't totally **butch**.

butt, n.
buttocks; *American*

> She had a **butt** you could serve tea on—and a Southern accent to match.

DERIVATION: Old English gives us the word *buttuc*, meaning ridge—as in the end of a piece of land. Which is what your butt is—the end of your personal landscape, for better or worse.

> I could make the whole of Manhattan disappear into [Jennifer Lopez's] amazing **butt**.
> —*David Copperfield*

butt floss, n.
thong underwear; *American*

> When I opened the broken stall door without knocking, I unexpectedly caught a glimpse of my boss pulling up his pink **butt floss**.

butt fuck, v.
to have anal sex; *American*

> **Butt fucking** may be messy, but it beats your average rim job any day.

butt pirate, n.
a man who takes pleasure in looting another man's booty; a homosexual man; *American*

> Make sure he's not a **butt pirate** or you'll be wasting your time, Marge.

Walking the Butt Plank

Seymore Butts directed the acclaimed (in certain circles) 2005 film *Butt Pirates of the Caribbean.*

butt slut, n.
promiscuous homosexual man; *American*

> Who are you calling a **butt slut**? I've only been with a couple dozen guys!

butter bags, n.
breasts; *American*

> If butter makes it better, let's grease up your **butter bags** and unzip my pants.

butter the muffin, v.
to copulate; *American*

> That Julia Child sure knew how to **butter the muffin**.

butterscotch chippy; n.

A lightly colored promiscuous woman; *American*

> When he went looking for sex, he sought out the **butterscotch chippies**.

---

buy bacon and eggs, v.

code for "I think this person is going to spend the night"; *American*

> On the way home, I'm going to stop to **buy some bacon and eggs**.

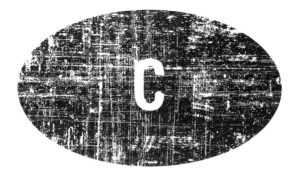

C2C, n.

homosexual anal intercourse; *American*

> Those buds were so close, they were **C2C**.

> **DERIVATION:** C2C is short for cock to cock.

caboose, n.

a woman with very large breasts; *American*

> With her DDs, Simone is a real **caboose**.

> **DERIVATION:** This term comes from the fact that a caboose follows her large breasts, which are naturally in the lead.

cack, n.

shit; *Irish*

> What a load of **cack**! Why would she ever want something put in that orifice?
>
> What a load of **shit**! Why would she ever want something put in that orifice?

> Marvin Acme. The rabbit **cacked** him last night.
> —*Who Framed Roger Rabbit?*

cafeteria, n.
orgy room; *American*

> I hear there's a **cafeteria** over on Vine if you're willing to eat out.

camel toe, n.
when a woman's tight pants go into her vagina and reveal the camel-toe-like shape; *American*

> Wardrobe Rule #1: The tighter the jeans, the more pronounced the **camel toe**.

Yeah, chicks go nuts for that
. . . the male **camel toe**.
—*Superbad*

candaulism, n.
sexual fetish in which a man enjoys displaying his partner in front of others; swinging; *American*

> My parents probably don't even know how to spell **candaulism**, but after I caught them in bed with the neighbors, they sure know how to do it.

candy apples, n.
a great ass; *American*

> I could bounce a quarter off that chick's **candy apples**.

candy wrapper, n.
someone who has been used; *American*

> She was my girlfriend. Now she's just a **candy wrapper**.

canine special, n.

the act of spreading peanut butter on one's penis and letting the dog lick it off; *American*

> The vet says little Rover is gaining too much weight—I think I should lay off the **canine special** for a while.

cans, n.

breasts; *American*

> Nice **cans**, sweetheart. Time to pop your top off.

cantaloupes, n.

breasts; *American*

> Some men prefer bananas, but I prefer **cantaloupes**.

Captain America, n.

a man who always carries a condom; *American*

> That Joe is a real **Captain America**.

Captain America, who is the famous character from the comic books published by Marvel Comics, always carried his shield for protection.

casting couch, n.

any piece of furniture on which a man of power seduces a woman with promises of advancement; *American*

> The photographer brought the model back to his studio and, after he promised to make her famous, she slept with him on the **casting couch**. She should have made him take the pictures first.

ABCDEFGHIJKLMNOPQRSTUVWXYZ

caught short, v.
to have to urinate; *British*

> I was **caught short** so I popped into the loo at the pub.

> I **had to pee** so I used the bathroom at the bar.

CBJ, n.
blowjob with condom; *American*

> Giving a **CBJ** is safer, but ugh, the taste?

celebrate the celibate, v.
to masturbate; *American*

> Every Friday night, I light a candle, say a prayer, and **celebrate the celibate**.

Centerville, n.
middle of a person's body where the genitals reside; *American*

> Sally and I went to **Centerville** last night.

chalk outline, n.
someone who isn't sexually responsive; *American*

> I got so tired of fucking the **chalk outline** that I switched to masturbation.

> **DERIVATION:** From the chalk outline that is used to represent a dead body at a crime scene.

champagne glasses, n.
small breasts; *American*

> My wife only sports **champagne glasses** but I don't mind.

chandelier, n.
a heavily ornamented woman; *American*

> Remember, a **chandelier** takes a lot of work to maintain.

charty, adj.
disgusting, gross; *Scottish*

> I'd snog you, but your breath is absolutely **charty**.

> I'd kiss you, but your breath is absolutely **disgusting**.

chased but chaste, adj.
attractive but holding out; *American*

> My sister is **chased but chaste**.

chav
ghetto (white) trash; from the Romany word *chavi*; *British*

> The council house across the street is full of **chavs**.

> The project across the street is filled with **ghetto trash**.

Of all the sexual aberrations, perhaps the most peculiar is **chastity**.
—*Remy De Gourmont, 1858-1915, French writer and philosopher*

check for dandruff, v.
study a person's genitals; *American*

> I watched this nature show on monkeys and just had to **check Alice for dandruff**.

cheeky, adj.
smartass; *British*

> Wipe that **cheeky** grin off your face and make me a sandwich!

> Wipe that **smartass** look off your face and make me a sandwich!

> Welcome back, my **cheeky** wee monkeys.
> —*Craig Ferguson*

cheesed off, v.
pissed off; *British*

> There's no reason to be **cheesed off** with me just because you caught me yanking my hard-on to your mom's picture.

> There's no reason to get **pissed off** at me just because you caught me masturbating to your mom's picture.

chem-friendly, adj.
prone to drug use; *American*

> There's no doubt the new guy I'm dating is **chem-friendly**—he showed up to our last dinner with bloodshot eyes smelling of stale weed.

cherry, n.
a sexual act that hasn't been performed by someone; *American*

> After dating for a year and a half, I finally popped her three-way **cherry**.

> Mr. Star, my **cherry** is obstructing my work. Sir, would you take it from me, free?
> —*Deadwood*

cherry dip, n.

sex while a woman is menstruating; *American*

> His idea of non-vanilla sex is to ask for a **cherry dip**.

chick with a dick, n.

transvestite; pre-sex change operation transsexual; *American*

> He thought she was hot until he realized she was a **chick with a dick**.

chicken counter, n.

someone who's sure he's getting laid; *American*

> Paul is a **chicken counter**. And he's counted wrong.

> **DERIVATION:** This expression comes from the proverb "Don't count your chickens before they're hatched."

chicken hawk, n.

older homosexual man who prefers younger partners; *American*

> The old queer down the hall? We call him Mr. **Chicken Hawk**, but I'm not sure what his real name is.

chicken pox, n.

desire for younger gay lovers; *American*

> It's either spring fever or I've got the **chicken pox**. There isn't a man in the room over twenty-five that piques my interest.

chili dog, n.

the act of a man defecating on a woman's breasts then tit fucking her, with his penis as the hot dog, the crap as the chili, and the breasts as the buns; *American*

> Pierre once lived next to a neighbor who was into **chili dogs** and proud of it; Pierre subsequently moved as soon as he could.

chill, v., adj.

to calm down; to be cool; American

> Charisma is seriously **chill**—she probably had a reason for kicking you in the balls.

chinless wonder, n.

snobby, rich man; *British*

> Look at that Porsche . . . no doubt driven by some **chinless wonder**.
>
> Look at that Porsche . . . no doubt driven by some **rich snob**.

chippy, n.

a promiscuous woman; *British*

> He cruised the streets looking for a suitable **chippy**.
>
> He cruised the streets looking for **an easy lay**.

> And here we have three more of Angel's **chippies**. You girls are on the pill, I hope.
> —*Angel*

chocolate bunny, n.

beautiful but empty; *American*

> Sure, she looks great, but she's a **chocolate bunny**.

chocolate chippy, n.

a darkly–colored, promiscuous woman; *American*

> When out looking for sex, I oddly have much better luck with **chocolate chippies**.

chode, n.

small penis; *American*

> Theresa left the **chodes** in the U.S. behind and moved to Kenya to indulge her fantasies.

choke the chicken, v.

to jerk off; *American*

> Bill was **choking the chicken** when his mother came home, so he hid in the pantry to finish up. It was a long night.

> You **choke the chicken** before any big date, don't you?
> —*There's Something About Mary*

choker, n.

large penis; *American*

> I can suck your acorn and an inch or two of shaft, but there's no way I'm getting all of that **choker** down my throat.

chremastistophilia, n.
sexual disorder in which pleasure is derived from being kidnapped or robbed; *American*

> Craig arranged for his landlord to break in one night and rob him blind while he masturbated, but sadly his insurance wouldn't pay for damages resulting from **chremastistophilia**.

chubby, n.
erection; *American*

> I stopped getting professional massages when I couldn't stop myself from getting a **chubby** each time the masseuse touched my feet.

My schedule, however, is as open as my relationship with my wife. So why don't we pair up? And hit the town together! I'll be your wingman. Even if it means me taking a **chubby**, I will suck it up!
—*Arrested Development*

chuffer, n.
jerk-off; *British*

> If he proposed but won't set a wedding date, your fiancé is a right **chuffer**.

If he proposed but won't set a wedding date, your fiancé is a real **jerk-off**.

DERIVATION: Chuffing is a common British term for masturbation.

churning butter, v.
fucking; *American*

> My girlfriend loves ice cream, but I prefer **churning butter**.

circle jerk, n.

a group of men who stand in a circle and either jerk each other off or masturbate; *American*

Stephan dropped by a friend's house with the understanding that there would be a **circle jerk** at his house, but when he got there, it was a baby shower instead. He should have kept his pants on.

Circle jerk of life. Where's the dignity?
—*The Sopranos*

the City, n.

Wall Street; *British*

My uncle is a hotshot banker in **the City** by day and an aspiring porn star by night. Same difference.

My uncle is a hotshot banker on **Wall Street** by day and an aspiring porn star by night. Same difference.

cleaning the kitchen, v.

rimming; *American*

Maybe after dinner we can **clean the kitchen**?

clear the desk, v.

what you say after sighting a coworker you want to fuck; *American*

Here comes Jess. **Clear the desk**.

cleft, adj.

a woman who has been energetically fucked; *American*

When I finally left my girlfriend's apartment, she was **cleft**.

clever dick, n.

obnoxious know-it-all; *British*

When you interrupt my story with what happens at the end, you're being a bloody **clever dick**.

When you interrupt my story with what happens at the end, you're being a fucking **obnoxious know-it-all**.

The Presidential Dick

The thirty-seventh president of the United States, Richard Millhouse Nixon, was such a clever dick that his nickname was Tricky Dick.

clit, n.

short for the clitoris; extremely sensitive area of a woman's vagina that can be sexually stimulated; *American*

By the time I found her **clit**, I was so drunk and exhausted I passed out right there.

DERIVATION: The clitoris goes by many names, but the clit word itself comes from the ancient Greek *Kleitoris*, which translates as "the man with the key." This surprisingly playful and perceptive derivation suggests that Greek women are happier than most.

Who Discovered the Clit?

Impossible as it may seem, men have been arguing over who discovered the clitoris for hundreds of years. The Italian physician Matteo Renaldo Columbo claimed his discovery of the "seat of a woman's delight" in 1559; his rival anatomist Gabriele Fallopius (yes, that Fallopius) protested this assertion, insisting that it was indeed he who had discovered the clitoris. Some one hundred years later, the Danish scientist Kaspar Bartolin debunked both men's claims, pointing out references to the clit that dated back to the second century. Of course, every woman knows that if anyone discovered the clit, it was Eve in the Garden of Eden.

All of my piercings, sixteen places on my body, all of them done with a needle. Five in each ear, one through the nipple on my left breast, one through my right nostril, one through my left eyebrow, one in my lip, one in my **clit** . . . and I wear a stud in my tongue.
—*Pulp Fiction*

clit fit, n.

emotional outburst; *American*

> Carl threw a real **clit fit** when he didn't get the iPod he wanted for his birthday.

clit sit, n.

a group of women talking and hanging out; *American*

> I can play late tonight; my girl's having a **clit sit**.

clone, n.

lover who resembles an ex; *American*

> It's kind of creepy that Walter is dating a **clone**.

closet door, n.

a woman who keeps a closeted homosexual husband from coming out, either because she wants to protect his image or to keep him from realizing his own homosexuality; *American*

> She's his cook, maid, and **closet door**.

closet freak, n.

someone in to sexual experimentation who seems completely "normal"; *American*

> I bet that librarian is a **closet freak**.

closet queen, n.

male homosexual who has not made public his sexuality; *American*

> I may have spent only five minutes talking to your fiancé, but I can tell you straight up, that is one serious **closet queen**.

clot, n.

moron; *British*

> The dickey-wearing Loren seemed sophisticated at first, but as soon as he opened his mouth, it was clear he was a **clot**.

> The dickey-wearing Loren seemed sophisticated at first, but as soon as he opened his mouth, it was clear he was a **moron**.

cluster fuck, n.

chaos created by a group of incompetents; *American*

> Every C-level management meeting is a **cluster fuck**.

DERIVATION: Also known as Charlie Foxtrot, a cluster fuck is a military term used to describe disastrous situations caused by too many inept commanding officers. The cluster refers to the oak-leaf shaped insignia worn by the brass.

> Well then, stick to it because you're a walking **cluster fuck** as an infantry officer. My men are hard chargers, Major! Lieutenant Ring and Gunny Highway took a handful of young fire pissers, exercised some personal initiative, and kicked ass!
> —*Heartbreak Ridge*

cock, n.

penis; *American*

> Steve's favorite T-shirt in college said, "Rock out with your **cock** out" and man, he got a lot of attention when he wore that thing to a party.

cock block, v.
blocking another person from having sex; *American*

> Just when the chick I had been trying to score with all night was sliding her hand down my pants, Al walked into the bedroom and **cock blocked** me.

cock dock, n.
male's sexual partner; *American*

> Robin is little more than a **cock dock**.

cock ornament, n.
a woman whose sole function is to be a sexual plaything; *American*

> She's not the love of my life, just a **cock ornament**.

cock snot, n.
semen; *American*

> Hand me a Kleenex, babe, I just got **cock snot** all over the sheets.

cock socket, n.
vagina; *American*

> Give me a minute to warm up my **cock socket** before we plug in the Sybian.

cock tease, n.

a woman who continually leads men to believe she will sleep with them, then changes her mind; *American*

> She told me all night how much she wanted to screw, but the **cock tease** left after drinks and dinner—and before dessert.

cockaholic, n.

woman or gay man addicted to sex; *American*

> Despite his brief stay in a treatment center, Nathan remains a **cockaholic**.

cock-a-thon, n.

frequent or numerous cases of sexual activity; *American*

> You'd never guess it, but with the invention of Viagra, my grandma's old folks' home is a regular **cock-a-thon**.

cocksucker, n.

derogatory term for a man who is inferior to oneself; a person who gives blowjobs; *American*

> That **cocksucker** better get his SUV out of my spot before I key his car.

> You can't cut the throat of every **cocksucker** whose character it would improve.
> —*Deadwood*

cocktail sauce, n.

semen that is ejaculated on a person's tailbone area; *American*

> If you're going to date Greg, you should prepare to have a lot of **cocktail sauce**.

> **DERIVATION:** This term comes from the cocktail sauce that is normally served with shrimp.

coconut, n.

Hispanic who acts Caucasian; *American*

> Mmm, I'd love to crack that handsome **coconut** in the polo shirt and Dockers in two and suck out all the sweet milk.

codswallop, n.

baloney; *British*

> Stop talking **codswallop** and blow me for fuck's sake!
>
> Stop talking **baloney** and blow me for fuck's sake!

> What a load of old **codswallop** this is.
> —*Are You Being Served?*

coffee roll, n.

sex with a dark-skinned lover; *American*

> For a change of pace, I like a **coffee roll**.

cojones, n.

balls; *American*

> Markus has a big set of **cojones**.
>
> **DERIVATION:** Cojones is the frequently used Spanish word for balls.

Egg-stra Special Slang

When it comes to swearing in the Hispanic-dominated California and Southwest, forget about *cojones*, here it's all about *huevos* (eggs), which is how balls are known. Eggs feature prominently in many slang expressions including: *¡A huevo!*, the hell it's right!, lit. to egg; *me importa un huevo,* I don't give a damn, lit. I care a ball (an egg); *and ¡Huevos!* Fuck you!, lit. balls!

> You bomb me with one more can, kid, and I'll snap off your **cojones** and boil them in motor oil!
> —*Home Alone*

coke, n.
cocaine; *American*

> Be sure to score a gram of **coke** before the Miley Cyrus concert—the music sucks if you're sober.

coked out, adj.
high on cocaine; *American*

> Now that I look back at my dad's erratic behavior, he was certainly **coked out** most of my childhood.

college thing, n.
a way to explain away something you once did . . . once; *American*

> Sure, I've slept with another woman, but that was just a **college thing**.

color in the coloring book, v.
masturbate to a pornographic magazine; *American*

> Since the age of ten when he discovered his dad's *Playboy* collection, Wayne has been **coloring in the coloring book**.

comarital, adj.
having extramarital affairs with a spouse's consent; *American*

> Tina is looking for a **comarital** relationship.

come the raw prawn, v.

to act naïve; to bullshit; *Australian*

> Don't **come the raw prawn** with me, Enid; I know you borrowed my bike without asking.

> Don't **bullshit** me, Enid; I know you borrowed my bike without asking.

cometosis, n.

bad breath after performing oral sex; *American*

> Please don't kiss me until you've brushed your teeth. It was nice to get a blowjob and all, but your **cometosis** is nauseating.

> **DERIVATION:** Cometosis is a combination of the words *come* and *halitosis*.

compass, n.

sexy woman; *American*

> That French woman's a **compass**.

> **DERIVATION:** From a compass having an arrow that points north (up).

concrete blonde, n.

prostitute; *American*

> My best friend's girlfriend was a **concrete blonde**, but he couldn't complain. After all, it paid the bills.

condom, n.

a contraceptive device made of latex worn on the penis;
American

> If you're out of **condoms** on Ladies Night, you're fucked
> (or not).

> **DERIVATION:** Odds are the term *condom* probably comes
> from the Latin word for container: *condos*. But there are
> those who insist that one enterprising seventeenth century
> Dr. Condom devised the sheath out of sheep gut to help His
> Royal Highness Charles
> II from spreading his,
> uh, seed throughout the
> land (Charles II, who had
> fathered at least fourteen
> illegitimate children at
> that time).

> A **condom** is the glass slipper
> for our generation. You slip one
> on when you meet a stranger.
> You dance all night, and then
> you throw it away.
> —*Fight Club*

condom distributor, n.

someone who sleeps around; *American*

> That quiet girl from school? Soon as she got out into the real world, she
> became a **condom distributor**.

controversy, n.

a new sexual practice; *American*

> I'm going to introduce a little **controversy** tonight.

convertible, n.
code for braless female; *American*

> There's a young **convertible** on your left.

....

coochie, n.
vagina; *American*

> That biddy was practically shoving her **coochie** in Ben's face, but he was completely oblivious and ended up going home alone.

Coochie Rap

The 2 Live Crew song "Pop That Coochie" is typical of the kind of music that came to be known as "booty rap" due to the graphic sexual nature of the lyrics. (Not to mention the title!)

....

cool your Joan Jetts, v.
a phrase used by men to emasculate each other, implying femininity; *American*

> So I told Michael, "Whoa there, missy, **cool your Joan Jetts**."

> Girls have got balls. They're just a little higher up, that's all.
> —*Joan Jett*

....

cooze, n.
vagina; *American*

> A **cooze** cruise to the Caribbean sounds like the perfect spring break getaway.

cooze ooze, n.
vaginal discharge; semen dripping from a vagina after sex; *American*

> The only bad thing about sloppy seconds is the **cooze ooze**.

coprophilia, n.

sexual compulsion involving feces; *American*

> My ex was totally into **coprophilia** and asked me to take a shit on his chest while I was blowing him. Gross.

cork the pork, v.

to have sex; *American*

> My husband is so classy. Last night he said, "Let's uncork the champagne and **cork the pork**."

cornhole, v.

to copulate; *American*

> Helen was your average naïve, milk-fed Midwestern farm girl until she went to college in Minneapolis and really learned how to **cornhole**.

cornhole, n.

anus; *American*

> And your doped-up bitches are gonna get sent back to Laos, and this fucking retard right here is gonna be testifying against you for a reduced sentence while you're getting **cornholed** by a gang of crackers.
> —*Gone Baby Gone*

> You put that thing in my **cornhole** by mistake and you'll never see me again.

DERIVATION: Back in the olden days before the invention of toilet paper, farmers used corn cobs or husks to wipe their cornholes.

cost big bikkies, v.

expensive; *Australian*

> My new iPhone **cost big bikkies**, but then again I went for the model that also doubles as a heart rate monitor, flashlight, and dildo.

> My new iPhone was **expensive**, but then again I went for the model that also doubles as a heart rate monitor, flashlight, and dildo.

cotton candy, n.

curly pubic hairs; *American*

> I love munching on Janice's **cotton candy**.

---

cougar, n.

an older woman (sometimes a MILF), over thirty-five, on the prowl for sex with younger men; *American*

> This **cougar** was hitting on Rich outside of a club, but started talking about her kid, so he booked it out of there.

Sexiest Celluloid Cougars

1. Anne Bancroft as Mrs. Robinson in *The Graduate*
2. Jennifer Coolidge as Stifler's Mom in *American Pie*
3. Ruth Gordon as Maude in *Harold and Maude*
4. Jane Seymour as Kitty Cat Cleary in *Wedding Crashers*
5. Jennifer O'Neill as Dorothy in *Summer of '42*

couldn't get a bunny pregnant, adj.

impotent; *American*

> He's had all that unprotected sex and he **couldn't get a bunny pregnant**.

DERIVATION: Rabbits are known for their reproductive abilities.

Cartoon Cursing

While Bugs Bunny may have been squeaky clean, Yosemite Sam had a mouth that could make a sailor blush. Examples of his wicked tongue include:

"Great horney toads!"
"Ooh, that rackin' frackin' rabbit."
"You dog-blasted, ornery, no-account, long-eared varmint!"

Cousin Itt, n.

a hairy pussy; *American*

On our third date, I finally got to take off her panties, but God damn if it wasn't **Cousin Itt** down there.

Cousin Itt was a character in the *Addams Family* television show who was completely covered in hair. Of course, that was the seventies and trends in pubic hair have changed. Nowadays who knows, Cousin Itt might be bald as a baby's bottom down there.

cow, n.

bitch; unattractive woman; *British*

His sister is a real **cow**, but, you know, I'd still slam it.

His sister is a real **bitch**, but, you know, I'd still hit it.

crack, n.

vagina; *American*

During biology class, my lab partner flashed her **crack** for no apparent reason.

crack salesman, n.

hustler; *American*

There's a **crack salesman** on every damn corner in this town. It sets a bad example for the grandkids.

crack whore, n.

crack-addicted female who sells her body for drugs; *American*

With her greasy hair and cum-stained dress, Susan looked more like a **crack whore** than a prom queen.

Let me show you Derelicte. It is a fashion, a way of life inspired by the very homeless, the vagrants, the **crack whores** that make this wonderful city so unique.
—*Zoolander*

cracker, n.

derogatory term for a white person; *American*

> That **cracker** on the Lakers can't play basketball to save his life.

> The white **cracker** who wrote the National Anthem knew what he was doing. He set the word free to a note so high nobody could reach it. That was deliberate.
> —*Angels in America*

crackerjack, adj.

shoddy; of poor quality; *American*

> When are you finally going to ditch that **crackerjack** phone and get an iPhone?

cracking, adj.

best; stunning; *British*

> I went home with a **cracking** girl last night and she ended up being a dirty slut.

> I went home with a **stunning** girl last night and she ended up being a dirty slut.

cracking an egg, v.

menstruating; *American*

> She's just moody because she's **cracking an egg**.

cracking Judy, n.

attractive woman; *American*

> Judge Judy was a real **cracking Judy**—something about a powerful, decisive woman with a hammer in her hand drives me absolutely wild.

crane, n.

an attractive person; *American*

> I drove past this **crane** and I thought my neck was going to snap.
>
> **DERIVATION:** This term comes from craning your neck to keep a hottie in sight.

crap, n., interj.

feces; *American*

> Holy **crap**! Take a look at the monstrous shit I just took.

> This is a bunch a **crap**! I've been licking this carpet for three hours and I still don't feel like a lesbian!
> —*South Park*

crapper, n.

toilet; *American*

> It's only been five minutes since I ate those taco supremes but I may be spending the next few hours on the **crapper**.

crave the wave, v.

to desire sex; *American*

> After two months with no sex, I **crave the wave**.

creak the bed, v.

to copulate; *American*

> Either we're having an earthquake or the neighbors are **creaking the bed** again.

cream, v.
to ejaculate; *American*

> I **creamed** on her face after sex, then went to sleep while she cleaned up. I never saw her again.

cream pie, n.
a vagina or asshole with sperm dripping from it; *American*

> We did it without a condom, and she had the messiest **cream pie** ever afterward.

creamsicle, n.
penis; *American*

> She wrapped her lips around his **creamsicle** and sucked til he was just an empty shell of a man.

> I could give you a Cambodian **creamsicle** . . . that will make you scream all night.
> —*Deuce Bigalow: European Gigolo*

crescent roll, n.
sex while one partner is wrapped in a blanket or sheet; *American*

> When Glen offered me a **crescent roll**, I thought he meant the Pillsbury kind.

crested, v.
to finally bag someone; *American*

> After four months of putting me off, I finally **crested** her.

crop dusting, v.

farting and walking simultaneously; *American*

> When I'm waiting in line and there are annoying people behind me, I end up **crop dusting** them with the hope that it will shut them up.

crotch crickets, n.

crabs; *American*

> For a nasty case of the **crotch crickets**, just soak your genitals in rubbing alcohol and set the little buggers on fire.

crotch rot, n.

sexually transmitted diseases; *American*

> Zara is such a ho that I can literally smell her **crotch rot** from across the room.

crowd pleasers, n.

breasts; *American*

> While she was breastfeeding, Karen always dressed to emphasize her engorged **crowd pleasers**.

crush hour, n.

last hour a bar is open to find someone to go home with for the night; *American*

> Listen up, it's **crush hour** and that skanky Goth is starting to look pretty damn good.

crusty, adj.

dirty; refers to a vagina; *American*

> When I started to go down on her, I discovered she was **crusty**.

CS, n.

clean shaven; *American*

> My only problem with her being **CS** is I think she gets help.

CSW, n.

slut; *American*

> She's my sister, so I can say honestly that she's a real **CSW**.
>
> **DERIVATION:** From Commercial Sex Worker, which is the politically correct term for prostitute.

cubicle, n.

a stall; *British*

> The corner pub has a nice loo with three **cubicles** if you need to take a shit.
>
> The corner bar has a nice bathroom with three **stalls** if you need to take a shit.

The Cubicle from Hell
Take a shit in a cubicle in America—and you'll get your ass fired.

cucumber queen, n.

someone who likes having vegetables placed in their orifices; *American*

> Robin is such a **cucumber queen** that I never eat salads over there.

cum, v.
to climax; a variation of "come" considered a more obscene spelling; *American*

> Harold always yells "Jesus, Mary, and Joseph!" when having sex; he says it helps him **cum**.

cumbunny, n.
young, sex-crazed woman; *American*

> From the way she fingers herself in that photo, your mom seems like a real **cumbunny**.

cumdumpster, n.
whore; vagina; *American*

> Did you see the tits on that **cumdumpster**?

cumshot, n.
ejaculation, usually on a woman's face, but can be on other body parts; *American*

> She still had some of my **cumshot** in her hair when we went out to dinner—it was a *There's Something About Mary* moment.

cunnilingus, n.
the act of performing oral sex on a woman; *American*

> We haven't seen **Colonel Angus** around these parts for years.
> —*Saturday Night Live*

> Carole never performs fellatio on her man unless he performs **cunnilingus** on her first—it's a tit for twat thing.

> **DERIVATION:** This Latin mouthful of a word comes from the happy marriage of the word *cunnus* (meaning vulva) and *linguere* (meaning to lick).

cunt, n.

a derogatory term for a woman; *American*

That **cunt** broke up with Ted by text message, and a second later, she accidentally sent him a message meant for the guy who she had also been seeing.

The Shock of It All

Considered by many to be one of the most offensive words in use in America, cunt was once described by feminist Germaine Greer as "one of the few remaining words in the English language with a genuine power to shock."

You're not a bad person. You're a terrific person. You're my favorite person. But every once in a while, you can be a real **cunt**. —*Kill Bill: Volume 2*

cunt-struck, adj.

obsessed with having sex with women or women in general; *American*

I had always considered myself straight as an arrow, but nevertheless, my first year at Mount Holyoke College was spent in a **cunt-struck** daze.

cupcake, v.

to snuggle or cuddle instead of going out to party; *American*

Friday night sucked—I wanted to get trashed at a frat party but my girlfriend just wanted to **cupcake** as usual.

cupcakes, n.

breasts; *American*

Jay hadn't squeezed the twinkie in a week so he was able to cream-fill her **cupcakes** in less than thirty seconds.

custard launcher, n.
penis; *American*

> Don't pig out at dinner—you've got to save room for my **custard launcher**.

....

cybersex, n.
Internet sex chat or activity; *American*

> **Cybersex** isn't cheating—it's just a little fun while the wife is out shopping.

....

> I tried to have **cybersex** once, but I kept getting a busy signal.
> —*You've Got Mail*

cyclops, n.
penis; vagina; *American*

> My goal tonight is to defeat a **cyclops**.

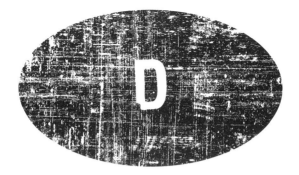

D train, n.
penis; *American*

> Hey baby, why don't you come for a ride? My **D train** is leaving for heaven in just a minute.

D&S, n.
dominance and submission; *American*

> The people next door are into **D&S**.

dacryphilia, n.
sexual arousal obtained by crying or tears, usually a male disorder; *American*

> I'm not sure if it's considered **dacryphilia**, but my husband insists on saying the most terrible things and making me cry before having sex.

dagger, n.
penis; *American*

> Jesus, watch where you swing that **dagger**. You could hurt someone!

dairy queen, n.

homosexual male of color who prefers whites; *American*

> There's a **dairy queen** in every town who's ready for fresh cream anytime.

daisy, n.

vagina; American

> Daisy Fuentes was my favorite **daisy**—I mean, va-jay-jay—I mean veejay.

daisy chain, n.

gay sex linked by oral and anal stimulation; *American*

> When spring is in the air and the flowers are blooming, my randy pink posse has an annual **daisy chain**.

dalmatian, n.

the act of painting a light-skinned person with feces; *American*

> When Mary said she was into **dalmatians**, I thought she meant the dog.

damn, v., n.

to curse, to condemn; a curse; *American*

> Frankly my dear, I don't give a **damn**.
> —*Gone With the Wind*

> When the priest says, "**damn** it all to hell," he really means it.

DERIVATION: This word comes to us from the Latin *damnare*, meaning to inflict loss upon.

dandy, n.
homosexual; *American*

I pursued Jason for months before I realized he was a **dandy**.

Who's the glad-handing **dandy**?
—*Twin Peaks*

dangler, n.
a woman with long pubic lips; *American*

Jeanne's a **dangler** if I've ever seen one—she can tie her lips in a knot.

dangly bits, n.
male private parts; *British*

Trust me, when my neighbor walks around his flat naked, you do not want to see his **dangly bits**.

Trust me, when my neighbor walks around his apartment naked, you do not want to see his **penis**.

Danish pastry, n.
a transsexual; *American*

Before you get too attached, you're looking at a **Danish pastry**.

DERIVATION: The first sex-change operation took place in Denmark, but they are now done at a reduced cost in Thailand, the sex mecca.

dark meat, n.
penis of color; *American*

I finally dumped that whitey Rob because whenever we fucked all I could think about was hot **dark meat**.

day-time drama, n.
sexual partner who isn't worth the trouble; *American*

> In bed, she's a tiger. Out of bed, nothing but a day-time drama.

deal from the bottom, v.
when a man performs intercourse up into a woman astride him; *American*

> I like it best when my man is **dealing from the bottom**.

debag someone, v.
to pants someone; *British*

> My first day in the dorms, a group of hooligans **debagged me**.

> My first day in the dorms, a group of bullies **pulled my pants down**.

declare war, v.
to have rough, angry sex with someone; *American*

> I knew my girlfriend was cheating on me, so before I dumped her, I **declared war** on her until she had trouble walking.

deep throat, v.
in oral sex, when one puts his entire penis down someone else's throat; *American*

> I saw a porn video where this girl **deep throats** an entire twelve-inch penis.

Chic, Chicer, Chicest

The 1972 movie *Deep Throat* was one of the first plot-driven porno films, giving rise to the term "porn chic." This groundbreaking X-rated flick asked the burning story question: How far does a girl have to go to untangle her tingle?

de-fag, v.

to rid one's surroundings of gay traits; *American*

> Before Zeke's preacher father came to visit, he had to **de-fag** his apartment by hiding anything questionable in the closet.

dendrophilia, n.

sexual disorder involving trees; *American*

> When my hairdresser said he had **dendrophilia**, I though he meant dandruff turned him on.
>
> **DERIVATIVE:** Literally dendrophilia means "love of trees" in Greek.

If It's Oak-ay with You, It's Oak-ay with Me

In ancient times, trees were fertility symbols worshipped by many. According to Brenda Love, author of *The Encyclopedia of Unusual Sex Practices*, men would even ejaculate on tree trunks to celebrate certain holy days. Finally, the source of the original woody.

derby, n.

fellatio; *British*

> I could use a **derby** right about now.
>
> I could use a **blowjob** right about now.
>
> **DERIVATION:** From the British derby hat, meaning head.

destroy, v.

to have angry, dominative sex; *American*

> She loved sex and also loved to be dominated; needless to say, I would **destroy** her on a nightly basis.

Minister: You may now kiss the bride.
Peter: Kiss her? I'm going to **destroy** her.
—*Family Guy*

ABCDEFGHIJKLMNOPQRSTUVWXYZ

dial 3825, v.

to copulate; *American*

For information, dial 411 and for copulation, **dial 3825**.

The 411 on 3825

Check the dial of any phone . . . 3825 represents the number/letter group which spells out *fuck*.

diamond studs, n.

hard nipples; *American*

He wasn't into rich bitches, but he did like a woman with **diamond studs**.

dibs, n.

the act of claiming someone or something so nobody else can take it; *American*

Marcus called **dibs** on that chick at the bar, and none of us said a word because he was pointing at a billboard of the Miller girls.

dick, n.

penis; a jerk; *American*

Dick is a **dick** with a nine-inch **dick**.

A Dick for Everyman

Dick is a variation of the Old English moniker Richard, so commonplace a name that it came to mean "Everyman"—and every man has a penis.

Hey, Ronald, I'm gonna go river boating on the Mississippi. I need something to measure depth. Can I borrow your **dick**?
—*Party Down*

dick around, v.

to do nothing of worth; to waste time; *American*

Murray shouldn't **dick around** as much with video games, or his girlfriend will dump him and he'll have to create a cyber girlfriend.

You wanna be in a band? Fine. Go ahead. Play every night. Play three times a night! Don't just **dick around** the same coffee house for five years.
—*Reality Bites*

dick hole, n.

a women whose sole function is sex; *American*

Three months ago, she was the love of his life. Now she's just a **dick hole**.

dickbeaters, n.

hands; *American*

The nuns always threatened us that jerking off would mean hairy **dickbeaters**, but they got that very, very wrong.

dickwad, n.

jerk; *American*

Not every Dick is a **dickwad**, but every **dickwad** is a dick.

Chill out, **dickwad**.
—*Terminator 2: Judgment Day*

dicky dunk, n.

sexual intercourse; *American*

Why don't you bring your donut over to my place for a little **dicky dunk** tonight?

ABCDEFGHIJKLMNOPQRSTUVWXYZ

diddle, v.
to have sex with; *American*

Despite my best intentions to remain faithful, I **diddled** my secretary every afternoon until wifey caught on.

diesel dyke, n.
a masculine lesbian; *American*

When Katrina slept with other women, she preferred a **diesel dyke** to a girly girl.

dig out, v.
to copulate; *American*

I **dug her out** like the ho she was.

dill doll, n.
dildo; *American*

She went straight from a Barbie doll to a **dill doll**.

DILLIGAF, n.
used to express intense disinterest; *American*

So you updated your profile. **DILLIGAF**.

DERIVATION: DILLIGAF is the acronym for "does it look like I give a fuck?"

dine at the Y, v.
perform cunnilingus; *American*

I'm going to **dine at the Y** during lunch.

ding dong, n.

penis; *American*

> If I had to do a movie star, it'd be King Kong—have you seen the size of his hairy **ding dong**?

Cream-Filled Fun

Hostess products have inspired several sexual slang terms. From the yellow Twinkie to the chocolate-covered Ding Dong, they have two things in common . . . a delicious cream filling and a shelf life of 100 years.

DINK, n.

a well-off couple with few to no family expenses; *American*

> No wonder Phyllis and Trevor both drive Jaguars and can afford to spend Christmas in Tahiti every year. What a bunch of **DINKs**.

I'm **Dink**, Bud **Dink**. You can call me Mister **Dink**!
—*Doug*

DERIVATION: DINK is an acronym for "double income, no kids."

dip the wick, v.

to have intercourse; *American*

> Did you **dip the wick** this weekend?

Dippoldism, n.

sexual disorder in which pleasure is derived from spanking or beating children; *American*

> After spending my childhood in Catholic school, I'd bet anything that half of nuns are into **Dippoldism**. The other half are just plain bitches.

dirty knees, n.

someone who gives oral sex; *American*

> Always act friendly to a woman with **dirty knees**.

dirty pillows, n.

breasts; *American*

> Let's take a bath together and soap up those **dirty pillows** of yours.

Dirty Sanchez, n.

an act where a man wipes his penis on a woman's upper lip to create a mustache after anal sex; *American*

> I love a woman with a mustache, so I gave her a **Dirty Sanchez**. She was not amused.

disposable number, n.

a one-night stand; *American*

> Go on, she's a **disposable number**.

ditch, n.

a woman who remains still during sex; *American*

> In public, a bitch. In bed, a **ditch**.

DNA, n.

anal sex; *American*

> The gay policemen got some good **DNA** at the crime scene.
>
> **DERIVATION:** This is an acronym for "dick 'n ass."

DnD, adj.

drug and disease free; *American*

> Per your request, here are the documents proving I'm **DnD**. Can we just go to bed now?

do it, v.

to have sexual intercourse; *American*

> As the song goes, birds **do it**, bees **do it**, even kiddiefucking priests **do it**—let's **do it**, let's fall in love.

do something that doesn't impact the environment, v.

to stay home and have sex; *American*

> Instead of driving to the mall to buy stuff we don't need, why don't we **do something that doesn't impact the environment**?

do the wild thing, v.

to copulate; *American*

> We **did the wild thing** in the wildest places—in an airplane, on the subway, and in the butthole.

ABCD**D**EFGHIJKLMNOPQRSTUVWXYZ

docking, n.
the sexual act of putting the head of the penis inside the foreskin of another man's penis; *American*

> Although he would never admit it, Benjamin was obsessed with **docking** to the point that it was the only way he would climax.

documentary, n.
a discreet signal to a friend that there is a sophisticated hot chick in ear range; sign to get a sophisticated girl's attention; *American*

> Did you see that **documentary** about that girl, I don't remember her name, but she had handlebars and always wore a striped shirt.

Create Your Own Buddy Codes

Since you aren't always free to point out a pair of visible nipples, you might want to create some code words so that you and your buddy never have to miss out.

- Create code words and not phrases— sure, it's very James Bond to say, "The swan flies low over the water," but by the time you finish, she's history.
- Select code words that stick out—if the code word for "stacked" is "afternoon," somebody is going to miss a lot of scenery.
- Select code words that make sense—if you're trying to be subtle, it's hard to throw the word "tyrannosaurus" into the mix without raising questions.

dodgy, adj.
not to be trusted; sketchy; *British*

> That Alec is right **dodgy**. He's always hitting on underage girls.

> Alec is really **sketchy**. He's always hitting on jailbait.

dog training, n.
a BDSM ("Bondage and Discipline, Sadism and Masochism") scenario where the submissive acts like a dog; *American*

> That quarterback from high school? Turns out he's into **dog training**. As the dog.

dogging, v.

having sex in public; *British*

> The long-married couple kept their sex life fresh by **dogging** in Central Park on their vacation in New York City. But no one even noticed.

> The long-married couple kept their love life fresh by **having sex in public** in Central Park on their vacation in New York City. But no one even noticed.

doggy style, adv.

sex from behind; *American*

> She had such a nice ass I just had to bend her over and give it to her **doggy style**.

donkey punch, v.

to punch someone in the back of the head during orgasm when having sex doggy style; *American*

> I once heard a story about a man who **donkey punched** a girl when they had sex and accidentally knocked her out. Now that's a cumcussion.

Congress of the Cow

The ancient sex manual known as the Kama Sutra describes several positions that feature what we think of as doggy-style fucking. The most famous of these is called the Congress of the Cow.

donkey rope, n.

penis; *American*

> **Donkey ropes** and asses go together like peanut butter and jelly.

donkey-rigged, adj.

possessing an enormous penis; *American*

> I wish my boyfriend were **donkey-rigged**. His tiny cock is nothing to write home about.

don't drop the soap, v.

watch out for the homosexuals; *American*

> If you join that team, **don't drop the soap**.
>
> **DERIVATION:** This term refers to a fear of bending over while in the shower with other men who might think you're presenting yourself.

---

donut puncher, n.

penis; homosexual male; *American*

> Mmm, put your **donut puncher** in my mouth and make me a Bavarian cream-filled.

So we're a **donut puncher**, after all?
—*Priscilla, Queen of the Desert*

---

doodie, n.

feces; *American*

> I can't bear the thought of making a **doodie** in a public toilet, so I always go at home before leaving the house.

---

doolally, adj.

crazy, eccentric; *British*

> That sexy, short girl I brought back to my flat was fucking **doolally** in bed.
>
> That pocket nymph I brought back to my apartment was fucking **crazy** in bed.
>
> **DERIVATION:** From *doolally tap*, meaning "camp fever."

Delusional Doolally

This expression comes from Deolali, India, where British forces were stationed during colonial times. Soldiers there suffered from a fever (likely malaria) that induced delusions while waiting for their homebound ships.

---

doorknob, n.

a buttplug shaped like a doorknob; *American*

> As uncomfortable as it was, Ed thought better a **doorknob** than a push bar.

doris, n.

girlfriend or wife; *British*

> We can actually go out and play pool tonight because my **doris** and her friends are watching *Sex and the City* for the millionth time.

> We can actually go out and play pool tonight because my **girlfriend** and her friends are watching *Sex and the City* for the millionth time.

dose, n.

veneral disease; *American*

> I thought she was a virgin until she gave me a **dose**.

double clicking the mouse, v.

female masturbation; *American*

> When I came home and saw my girlfriend **double clicking the mouse** while staring at herself in a mirror, I thought, "I really want to have sex with that narcissist."

double fisting, n.

the act of fisting with both hands (putting both hands inside someone's vagina or anus); *American*

> He can't walk a straight line because he's obsessed with **double fisting**.

Double fisting can also refer to carrying a glass of beer in each hand at the same time. That's why your chances of double fisting your girlfriend double if she's been double fisting beer the whole night.

double header, n.

69 between two gay males; fellatio twice in the same day; *American*

> Fran liked sucking Tony off at first, but got sick and tired of weekend **double headers** after just a few weeks.

> **DERIVATION:** Double header is a baseball term for two games back to back.

America's Favorite Pastime

Baseball terms abound in the world of slang. From *balls* to *second base* to *batting for the other side*, it's clearly a sport for the sexually adventurous.

double shot, n.

ejaculating twice during sex; *American*

> I didn't think coming twice was possible for a man until my boyfriend had a **double shot**.

double wedding, n.

the 69 position; *American*

> We may have eloped, but now we're into **double weddings**.

double-bagger, n.

Someone you have sex with despite their unattractiveness; *American*

> I was so desperate I made a move on a **double-bagger**.

double-bedder, n.

a woman so fine that you want two mattresses under her to cushion the pounding; *American*

> My hot blind date turned out to be a **double-bedder**.

double-header, n.
a woman who gives you oral sex, vaginal sex, and then finishes you off in her mouth; *American*

> My girlfriend is such a **double-header** that she must like her own taste.

double-sided form, n.
someone who likes vaginal and anal sex; *American*

> Then again, I don't mind filling out a **double-sided form**.

douche bag, n.
an unkind or unthoughtful person; *American*

> That **douche bag** in the Porsche who cut us off? I followed him home and keyed his car.

douchepacker, n.
a lesbian who wears a strap-on dildo to have sex with other women; *American*

> Maxine is into chicks, just not **douchepackers**.

Beth McIntire is from a whole 'nother planet, bro. I mean, she's beautiful, she's charming. As for you, I mean, I love you and all but let's face it: you're kind of a **douche bag**.
—*Cloverfield*

You just take Katrina the **douchepacker** to prom. I'm sure you two will have like a real bitchin' time.
—*Juno*

downtown, n.
vagina; *American*

> Sorry, I'd keep away from going **downtown** today—I'm on the rag.

DP, n.
double penetration; *American*

> You want to feel full? Try **DP**.

dream of cream, v.
to have a wet dream; *American*

> When I dream of Jeannie, I **dream of cream**.

dress for sale, n.
a prostitute; *American*

> Last night I saw a **dress for sale** just outside H&M.

dripping for it, adj.
horny; *American*

> Is that pussy juice on your thigh? Wow, you're literally **dripping for it** aren't you?

drive while parking, v.
to give oral sex to a man behind the wheel; *American*

> After leaving the movie theater, they **drove while parking**.

drop one's drawers, n.
to pull down one's underwear; *American*

> **Drop your drawers** and bend over so we can just get the honeymoon over with.

dry humping, v.
frottage; rubbing of genitals, usually with clothes on; *American*

Bobby and I weren't ready to lose our virginity but I was hornier than a nun on Easter, so we settled on **dry humping**.

A hug is just like a public **dry hump**.
—*How I Met Your Mother*

DSL, n.
dick sucking lips; *American*

That biddy over there has incredible **DSL** and I'm quite willing to accommodate her every wish for a blowjob.

dual airbags, n.
breasts; *American*

I didn't mind bumping into Susan, especially considering her **dual airbags**.

duck butter, n.
sweat that accumulates in between a man's scrotum and anus; *American*

It's so hot in here I could practically wring out my boxers from all this **duck butter**.

dude, n.
informal way to address another male in a positive way; *American*

Dude, I call dibs on that chick, except if she's a lesbian—then she's all yours.

Let me explain something to you. Um, I am not "Mr. Lebowski." You're Mr. Lebowski. I'm the **Dude**. So that's what you call me. You know, that or, uh, His **Dudeness**, or uh, **Duder**, or El **Duderino** if you're not into the whole brevity thing.
—*The Big Lebowski*

DUFF, n.

acronym for "designated ugly fat friend"; *American*

Sorry, but I called dibs on the blonde; you're stuck with the **DUFF**.

dugout canoe, n.
penis; *American*

It must be my Native American heritage—I've always wanted to take Pocahontas for a ride in my **dugout canoe**.

dumbass, n.
idiot; *American*

Tell that **dumbass** brother of yours to keep his comments to himself.

dump, v.
to break up with someone; *American*

Sure, I **dumped** her because she didn't understand *Battlestar Galactica*, but it was a perfectly rational decision at the time.

dunk, n.
fuck; *American*

I'm full of energy—had a **dunk** before coming into work today.

dust under the bed, v.

to have energetic sex that spills over onto the floor; *American*

Last night, we decided to **dust under the bed**.

Dutch girl, n.

lesbian; *American*

Grover wasted half the night buying drinks for a **Dutch girl**.

DERIVATION: Pun on dike (common in Holland) and dyke (lesbian).

dyke, n.

lesbian; *American*

Ellen's wife has to be the hottest **dyke** in Hollywood.

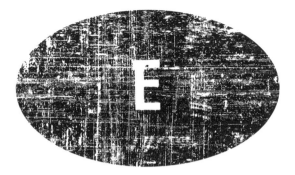

eagle wings, n.
when a woman's legs are spread wide open; *American*

> I walked into the bedroom to see **eagle wings**.

earmuffs, n.
a woman's thighs; *American*

> I prefer my **earmuffs** without stubble.

> **DERIVATION:** Earmuffs comes from thighs which cover the ears during oral sex.

earn one's red wings, v.
to perform cunnilingus on a woman while she's menstruating; *American*

> Creed **earned his red wings**, all right—he pulled his girlfriend's tampon out with his teeth and spent an hour down there.

earthquake, n.
sex that knocks things over or off the wall; *American*

> We had us an **earthquake** last night.

eat at home, v.
to have sex with your usual partner; *American*

> After a string of affairs, he found he enjoyed **eating at home**.

eat me, interj.
no way; not a chance; *American*

> You want to borrow another fifty bucks? **Eat me**!

It is not possible to **eat me** without insisting that I sing praises of my devourer?
—*Fyodor Dostoevsky*

eat shit, v.
to humble yourself; *American*

> Whenever Darlene has had enough of her boss, she tells him to "**eat shit** and die." She's had five jobs in two years.

eat someone out, v.
to perform cunnilingus; *American*

> I was in the mood for pizza but to save money we stayed in and I **ate** Elaine **out** instead.

ecofreak, n.
strict environmentalist; *American*

> I have some wood that could be saved by that **ecofreak**.

edger, n.
a trimmed bush; *American*

> My ex-girlfriend's girlfriend has an **edger**.

edging, v.
coming close to orgasm then backing off; *American*

> After two hours of **edging**, I worked up to a mind-blowing orgasm that brought tears to my eyes . . . and hers.

Edging is used in tantric sex to abstain from ejaculation while permitting intense orgasm.

edibles, n.
edible underwear; *American*

> I wonder if **edibles** are fat-free.

educating myself, n.
watching porn; *American*

> Jerry is upstairs **educating himself**.

> **DERIVATION:** From the notice at the beginning of many pornographic movies touting their educational value.

effie, n.
effeminate gay male; *American*

> I couldn't believe Sandra was hitting on that **effie**.

ego surf, v.

to surf the Internet looking for one's own name; *American*

> Andrew is so driven to be e-famous that he spends half of the day posting and the other half **ego surfing** for his posts.

Eiffel Tower, n.

an erect penis that's much thicker at the base; *American*

> As a high school exchange student, I spent a year saying ooh-la-la to Pierre's **Eiffel Tower**.

Eiffel Tower, n.

the sexual act of a man or woman receiving doggy-style sex from one guy and blowing another guy while those two guys are high-fiving; *American*

> My friends and I decided we wanted to do the **Eiffel Tower**, but couldn't decide on which person would do what, so it never materialized.

eight-pager, n.

graphic pornography; *American*

> The IT guy keeps an **eight-pager** in his desk at work.

> **DERIVATION:** In the 1930s and '40s, an eight-pager was a pornographic book that could easily be carried in a pocket.

ejac vac, n.

someone who gives blowjobs; *American*

> Robin is a real **ejac vac**.

> **DERIVATION:** Ejac vac is short for someone who vacuums ejaculations.

electile dysfunction, n.

the incapability to be aroused by any presidential candidates; *American*

Ralph made it to the booth to cast his vote, but then he suffered spontaneous **electile dysfunction** and immediately had to leave without casting his wad.

Electile dysfunction affects millions. But going early is completely natural. It happens to a lot of men.
—*The Daily Buzz*

elevator, n.

licking your way up or down a partner; *American*

This **elevator** stops at every floor, so I hope you washed behind your ears.

emo, n.

a form of punk rock known for its mildly pornographic, depressive, melodramatic lyrics; *American*

You'll know **Emo** Eddie when you see him; he's got that curtain of black hair falling across his face and "Pretend You're Alive" by Lovedrug on his iPod blaring in his ears.

We're not goth, we're **emo**.
—*St. Trinian's*

end table, n.

an ass that could support a glass; *American*

Seeing that my girlfriend was talking to someone else, I set my beer on her **end table**.

endytophilia, n.

preference for having sex with fully clothed partners; *American*

That 300-pound girl with the glasses? I'd do her only if I could be into **endytophilia** for the day.

Energizer bunny, n.
a sexual partner who takes forever to cum; *American*

> I got about two hours of sleep last night, just what I deserve for being married to the **Energizer bunny**.

ephebophilia, n.
sexual disorder involving attraction to adolescents and/or teenagers; *American*

> If I had a dollar for every man that fantasized about screwing a Catholic schoolgirl, I'd have enough to fund the world's largest **ephebophilia** foundation.

escort, n.
prostitute; *American*

> Since Bobby was new to town, he called an **escort** service rather than waste time looking for chicks.

eve teasing, n.
the act of frotteurism on an unsuspecting woman; *American*

> Priyanka didn't mind riding the commuter train to downtown Delhi each morning, but the **eve teasing** jerks that hung around the station were a real pain.

> **DERIVATION:** Eve teasing is a popular expression in India.

examine her tonsils, v.
fuck her face; *American*

> Sometimes at doctors appointments I fantasize about him **examining my tonsils**.

exchange body fluids, v.

to have sex; *American*

> In order to **exchange body fluids,** you've normally got to exchange numbers first.

ex-gay, n.

former homosexual; *American*

> Geoff put his faith in his church and attended intensive re-education sexual orientation training sessions run by an **ex-gay** to "cure" his homosexuality.

ex-hole, n.

combination of ex and asshole; *American*

> Two **ex-holes** later, I finally gave up marriage for good.

explore the map of Tasmania, v.

to copulate; *Australian*

> Hugh Jackman has got to be the sexiest Australian actor—I'm not a big traveler, but I wouldn't say no to **exploring the map of Tasmania** with him.

> Hugh Jackman has got to be the sexiest Australian actor—I'm not a big traveler, but I wouldn't say no to **copulating** with him.

extravadraganza, n.

drag queen show; *American*

> And now, ladies and ladies, it's time for the **extravadraganza** to begin!

eye candy, n.

a very attractive person; *American*

> That biddy was pure **eye candy**, so hot she could melt everything in the frozen food section with just a look.

eye of the storm, n.

vagina; *American*

> They say when the **eye of the storm** reaches its climax, it can interfere with the motion of the ocean.

Yeah, yeah, yeah, that's it. While you were cooking, you know, he was watching one of those, uh, those, uh, telenovels, y'know, with all those ripe honeys on it? Y'know, he was really into it. I told you not to change the channel, man! Y'know, dude needs his **eye candy**. That's it!
—*Breaking Bad*

eye sex, n.

undressing each other with the eyes; *American*

> When Teresa and Eric looked at each other for the first time, that look lasted long enough to make him hard and her wet. **Eye sex** led inevitably to intercourse—and they have been together ever since.

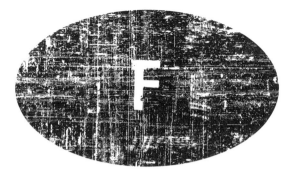

face base, n.
when a relationship has matured to the point that it is posted on one's Facebook profile; *American*

> Tamara was a hottie, but I figured if we hadn't made it to **face base** by our third date, it wasn't worth pursuing.

face fuck, v.
when receiving oral sex, a man thrusting as though actually having intercourse with his partner's mouth; *American*

> **Face fucking** is easier on those without a gag reflex.

face job, n.
ejaculation on a partner's face; *American*

> I thanked her for the blowjob with a **face job**.

facial, n.
the act of receiving sperm on one's face; *American*

> I got a **facial** only once, but it's true that despite the sickening smell my skin was soft and supple for days afterward.

factory-equipped, adj.

pre-op transsexual with all their original genitalia; *American*

> That "guy" is **factory-equipped**—she may have removed her breasts but down there you'll still find a tasty hair pie.

fade, n.

gay male of color who prefers lighter skinned males; *American*

> Come on, Rob, you're tanned enough to know that you don't have a chance with Finn; he's a total **fade**.

fag stag, n.

straight male who associates mostly with gay males; *American*

> Since the show *Queer Eye for the Straight Guy*, the number of **fag stags** has increased dramatically.

fag(got), n.

homosexual; *American*

> Tobias came into work wearing a pink shirt the other day—what a closet **fag**.

faghag, n.

a woman with mostly homosexual friends; *American*

> Charlotte is a classic **faghag**—a straight, boyfriend-less thirty-something who spends all her free time at gay bars with her queer friends.

fair dinkum, adj.
the real McCoy; genuine; *Australian*

> Wait, her lady-bazzers are **fair dinkum**? No bloody way!

> Wait, her tits are **genuine**? No fucking way!

fairy, n.
homosexual; *American*

> Your brother is a huge Judy Garland fan? Judging from his taste in music, I'd say he's a **fairy**.

> You know pumpkins . . . sometimes it just takes a **fairy**.
> —*To Wong Foo Thanks for Everything, Julie Newmar*

fairy godmother, n.
gay man's mentor; *American*

> I waited until I was thirty to come out of the closet, and asked my **fairy godmother** for help explaining things to my family.

fancy, v.
to desire; *British*.

> I **fancy** the pants off her.

> I'd **like** to get her in bed.

> Some desire is necessary to keep life in motion, and he whose real wants are supplied must admit those of **fancy**.
> —*Samuel Johnson*

fanny, n.
butt; *American*

> With a **fanny** like hers, the term fanny pack takes on a whole different dimension.

That's Fanny to You
Outside of the United States, fanny can also mean pussy, so think twice before you throw your fanny around overseas.

faygele, n.
gay; *American*

> Oy gevalt, my grandson the doctor—a **faygele**. What a pity.
>
> **DERIVATION:** Faygele comes from the Yiddish vögele, for "little bird."

FB, n.
fuck buddy; someone you meet for casual sex; *American*

> Rodney, the new guy who just moved in upstairs, is a potential **FB**.

FedEx, n.
premature ejaculation; *American*

> He said he wanted to make love all night and then pulled a **FedEx**.
>
> **DERIVATION:** FedEx provides speedy delivery anywhere in the world, anytime.

feed the kitty, v.
to have sexual intercourse; *American*

> Here puss puss, daddy wants to **feed the kitty**.

feel rougher than a badger's arse, v.
to be hung over; *British*

> After the drunken escapades of my twenty-first birthday, I woke up **feeling rougher than a badger's arse** and puked up the eggs and bacon that my mum made for me.
>
> After the drunken escapades of my twenty-first birthday, I woke up **hung over** and puked up the eggs and bacon that my mom made for me.

felching, n.

the act of licking fresh semen out of a vagina or anus; *American*

> I suck a mean dick and I'm not afraid to swallow, but **felching** just doesn't appeal to me.

Felicia, n.

gay man who performs fellatio frequently; *American*

> I wouldn't trade my pretty little **Felicia** for the biggest cock in town, no sir.

fellatio, n.

polite term for a blowjob; *American*

> She was a high-class girl, so she actually used the term **fellatio** when she asked me if I'd like a blowjob.

> She thinks **fellatio** is a character in Shakespeare.
> —*Cherry Falls*

DERIVATION: Inevitably, this term comes from the Latin *fellare*, meaning "to suck." Depending on who's sucking whose dick, you may be a:

- fellatrix: woman performing fellatio on a man
- fellatrice: woman performing fellatio on a man
- fellator: man performing fellatio on another man

ferret, n.

penis; *American*

> Why don't we set up a playdate for my pet **ferret** and your beaver?

fey, adj.

gay; effeminate; *American*

> No need to play so coy with me, I can see you're **fey** from a mile away.

fierce, adj.

cool; ferocious; *American*

> Your patent boots are **fierce**! Did you get them at Bergdorf's?

FILO, n.

a virgin who marries the first person they sleep with; *American*

> Sharon was a **FILO**. I'm set for life.

> **DERIVATION:** Who says accountants can't talk sexy? This term is finance jargon for "first in, last out."

filth, n.

police, pigs; *British*

> Watch out, I smell bacon so that must mean the **filth** are somewhere nearby.

> Watch out, I smell bacon so that must mean the **police** are somewhere nearby.

F.I.N.E., adj.

acronym for "fucked up, insecure, neurotic, and emotional"; *American*

> Gwen went from fine to **F.I.N.E**. after just a year of marriage.

fingering, n.

the act of inserting a finger into a vagina or anus for sexual pleasure; *American*

Hold That Shot

In the Kama Sutra, a man who suffers from premature ejaculation is advised to caress his lover's clitoris with his fingers to the point of orgasm before penetration.

> The art of **fingering** is one every young man should master—and every young woman should enjoy.

If you need me, just call. You know how to dial, don't you? You just put your **finger** in the hole and make tiny little circles.
—*Dead Men Don't Wear Plaid*

firehose, n.
penis; *American*

> Firemen are known for their muscular physiques, prompt service, and long **firehoses**.

fish, n.
derogatory gay slang for a straight woman; *American*

> Ugh, I can smell that **fish** from across the room. Someone should tell her to close her legs.

fish flaps, n.
labia; *American*

> Spread your **fish flaps** and let old Gorton try for a catch, eh?

fish stick, n.
penis; *American*

> I could smell her pink oyster from a mile away, but slammed my **fish stick** in nonetheless.

fit bird, n.
hot chick; *British*

> Let's get drunk, guys, and see who can kiss a **fit bird** in this pub. (Because **fit birds** just love drunk guys hitting on them.)

> Let's get drunk, guys, and see who can kiss a **hot chick** in this bar. (Because **hot chicks** just love drunk guys hitting on them.)

flaming, adj., flamer, n.

homosexual; *American*

> Our high school drama teacher had a girlfriend for years, but we all knew that **flamer** would come out of the closet someday.

flapjacks, n.

small female breasts; *American*

> I'd like to pour me some syrup on those **flapjacks**.

flash git, n.

showoff; *British*

> I don't know why Sue likes that **flash git**—he literally was wearing a bright yellow jumpsuit and dancing like he was at a disco.

> I don't know why Sue likes that **showoff**—he literally was wearing a bright yellow jumpsuit and dancing like he was at a disco.

flash in the pan, n.

one who is quick to ejaculate; *American*

> Yes, to tell you the truth I'm disappointed you didn't last long. I didn't sit through another showing of *Star Wars* for a **flash in the pan**.

flash the V, v.

to show the vagina; *American*

> This hot biddy named Tamora kept **flashing her V** to me while we were going over *Titus Andronicus* in my English class, which is just inappropriate on a whole other level. I'd still destroy that girl though.

> **DERIVATION:** In Britain, flash the V means to "flip the bird," so a particularly vulgar girl could flash the V twice at the same time.

flatulophilia, n.

sexual arousal derived from farting; *American*

> Homer Simpson may not be a hunk, but Marge is into **flatulophilia,** so it's all good.

flesh bombs, n.

breasts; *American*

> Keep your bra on and those **flesh bombs** on standby, okay?

fleshlight, n.

a male sex toy, shaped like a flashlight, that is used for masturbation; *American*

> After my roommate Boris bought a **fleshlight**, I didn't see him leave his room for two straight days.

"V" Is For . . .

The V sign in all its fingered variations (palm in, palm out, etc.) around the world can mean a number of wildly different things to different people:

- *Peace,* as in the "peace sign" popularized in the 1960s
- *Victory,* as used by Winston Churchill in World War II to encourage a besieged people
- *The letter "V,"* as employed in American Sign Language
- *The number 2,* when counting on your fingers
- *Air quotes,* a gesture with both hands that indicates putting a spoken word in quotes
- *Flipping the bird,* primarily in the United Kingdom
- *The Devil,* when placed behind an unsuspecting person's head as "devil's horns"

flip collar fairy, n.

gay clergyman; *American*

> As an altar boy, I loved my duties but kept a close eye out for the **flip collar fairies**.

flip-flop, v.

to perform both roles as a "top" and a "bottom"; *American*

> Always aiming to please his partner, Claude **flip-flopped** on a regular basis.

flip one's bitchswitch, v.

when a woman loses her temper; *American*

> It was just a measly little one-night stand, but when my wife found out she **flipped her bitchswitch**.

flippin', adj., adv.

term used to censor "fucking" in the song lyrics of *Flight of the Conchords*; *British, New Zealand*

> I sometimes say to people that I am in fact the mother **flippin'**. Rhymenocerous, but they don't get my reference to *Flight of the Conchords*.

> I sometimes say to people that I am in fact the mother **fuckin'**. Rhymenocerous, but they don't get my reference to *Flight of the Conchords*.

float an air biscuit, v.

to fart; *British*

> That bloody dog just **floated air biscuits**. He stinks!

> That damn dog just **farted**. He stinks!

floss her teeth, v.
receive a blowjob; *American*

> After dinner, I'm going to **floss her teeth**.

flow, n.
menstruating; *American*

> My dog is on the **flow**, so don't let your mangy mutt near her.

fluff the muff, v.
to masturbate a woman; *American*

> Richard had only one redeeming quality; he liked to **fluff the muff**.

fluffer, n.
porn movie assistant who is responsible for orally stimulating male cast members if their erections fail; *American*

> My childhood dream was to be a **fluffer**, but I decided on urology instead—just as many dicks but with a six-figure income.

fly fishing, v.
fondling a man's genitals; *American*

> If Otis decides on **fly fishing** one of our friends for a joke, he better make sure his victim isn't bigger than him.

foam, n.
ejaculation; *American*

> I spewed **foam** all over my favorite Starbucks barista on our first date.

fog up the windows, v.
to have sexual intercourse in a vehicle; *American*

> Tonight me and my girl are going to **fog up the windows**.

> **DERIVATION:** From the condensation from heavy breathing in an enclosed space.

fork and spoon, n.
69; *American*

> Then we had a little **fork and spoon** action.

formicophiliac, n.
sexual fetish involving insects, usually letting insects crawl on the body; *American*

> Dan and I spent a **formicophiliac's** ideal afternoon trapping bugs under glasses and watching them fight to the death, then fucked each other's brains out.

forty-niner, n.
a cross-gender person whose true gender is obvious; *American*

> Oh, please. She's from LA, but is clearly a **forty-niner**.

fourgy, n.
foursome usually involving two men and two women; *American*

> My top fantasies are: 1) a **fourgy**, 2) an orgy, and 3) that my boyfriend gets a job.

four-poster bed, n.

code that someone is into bondage; *American*

> I thought she was vanilla until she mentioned her **four-poster bed**.

....

frak (or frack), v.

term used on television show *Battlestar Galactica* to censor the word "fuck"; *American*

> **Frak** you, if you don't watch *Battlestar Galactica* like it's your religion.

....

frankenfood, n.

food that has been genetically modified; *American*

> You know the world has been turned upside down when **frankenfood** has taken over and strawberries contain fish genes to prevent frost.

> Well quite frankly, I don't give a flying **frak** whether you believe me or not! Because I've had it. I am—I am tired of being pushed and prodded around like I'm some kind of toy. I'm not your plaything!
> —*Battlestar Galactica*

....

frankfurter, n.

penis; *American*

> When my girlfriend entered the hot dog eating contest, my **frankfurter** was practically screaming for a little relish.

to freak, v.

to copulate; *American*

> Every time my girlfriend and I **freak** each other's brains out, she insists on playing speed metal.

French, v.

to kiss using the tongue; *American*

> I was expecting Jack to kiss me after our date, but certainly wasn't expecting him to **french** my ear.

French dressing, n.

semen; *American*

> I don't really care for **French dressing**, but have eaten it many times out of politeness' sake.

French embassy, n.

any establishment frequented by homosexuals; *American*

> For a delicious coffee and excellent Danish pastries, try the **French embassy** around the corner.

French kiss, n.

openmouthed kiss; *American*

> On the French class trip, everyone spent the afternoon at the Louvre but I spent my time sharing **French kisses** with Laurent.

French virgin, n.

someone who won't sleep with you because of a false sense of superiority; *American*

> Jen's not pure, she's just a **French virgin**.

friar, n.
fuck; *British*

> Rachel's a total bastard to her fiancé and he doesn't give a **friar**.

> Rachel's a total douche bag to her fiancé and he doesn't give a **fuck**.

friend of Dorothy, n.
gay male; *American*

> Any **friend of Dorothy** is a friend of mine.

> **DERIVATION:** In the movie *The Wizard of Oz*, Dorothy was played by Judy Garland, a gay icon.

friends with benefits, n.
two friends who have sex, but aren't in a romantic relationship; *American*

> Maurice and Noreen became **friends with benefits**, until Noreen started crying every time after they had sex, and so now they're just friends with awkwardness.

> You'll be happy to know that I now have a much better understanding of **"friends with benefits."**
> —*The Big Bang Theory*

frighten the chipmunks, v.
have outdoor sex; *American*

> Over the weekend, we **frightened the chipmunks** in the city park.

frighten the horses, v.
to exhibit overt sexuality; *American*

> Try dressing down tonight when we visit my parents; you don't want to give the impression that you **frighten the horses**.

front; bottom, n.
vagina, crotch; *British*

> When I was in my bikini, Jeff wouldn't stop complimenting me on my **front bottom**, the fucking pervert.

> When I was wearing my bikini, Jeff wouldn't stop complimenting me on my **crotch**, the fucking pervert.

front marriage, n.
a marriage between a gay and lesbian to get health benefits and other rights when afforded only to married couples in their states; *American*

> When Harriet got breast cancer, she took up her gay friend Glenn's thoughtful offer to have a **front marriage** so she could get the treatment options his health plan offered.

frotteurism, n.
the perversion of rubbing up against someone for sexual pleasure; *American*

> Those crazy French may have invented the term **frotteurism**, but the old Japanese businessmen rubbing up against schoolgirls in packed commuter trains have really taken it to the next level.

frozen meat, n.
dildo; *American*

> Sharon spent the night trying to thaw a piece of **frozen meat** that she'd left outside on the patio table.

> **DERIVATION:** From the hard nature of dildos, with meat as another word for the penis.

fruit cup, n.

jockstrap; *American*

> Boxers don't do a thing for me, but my hubby's **fruit cup** really turns me on.

fruit fly, n.

a man who only has homosexual sex while traveling; *American*

> Not only is Ralph a **fruit fly**, but he also tries to write off his activities as a business expense.

fruit fly, n.

straight woman who associates mostly with gay males; *American*

> When the **fruit flies** descend on us, just wave them away forcefully.

FTM, n.

female to male transsexual; *American*

> It may not be as easy as a snip-snip, turn it inside out, but it is indeed possible to create a penis from a vagina for a deserving **FTM**.

fuck, v.

to have sex; *American*

> To **fuck** or to make love, that is the question upon which many a relationship may ultimately flounder.

Food for Thought

Many of our evocative words for fruits and vegetables are sexual in origin (the very word fruit can refer to the child borne of a sexual coupling):

- Avocado comes from the Aztec word *ahuacatl*, meaning testicle.
- Vanilla comes from the Latin word *vaina*, meaning vagina.
- Tomato comes from the Nahautl word *tomatl*, meaning swelling fruit.
- Carrot comes from the Greek *karoton*, meaning horn.
- Fig comes from the Latin *fic*, which as slang could mean vagina, due to the resemblance to female anatomy when cut in half.

The Incredible, Iconic Fuck

Fuck is arguably the most versatile and functional obscenity in the English language. The many fucking ways in which you fuckers can fuck with the word fuck are unfuckingbelievable.

DERIVATION: The word fuck is nearly as old as, well, fucking itself. Some say it comes from the Greek word *phu,* which means to "plant seeds." Under the Romans it became *fu,* as in *fututio.* That is, the repeated planting of seed after seed in a furrow. Some say that the word fuck most likely comes from the Old German *fuk,* meaning "to strike," related to the Dutch *fokken,* meaning "to thrust," and the Swedish *fock,* meaning "penis."

Roman Poetry Slam

The Roman word *futuo* was the poetic fuck of its day. A favorite of the erotic poets, you'll find it throughout the most licentious lyrics of the time:

*sed domi maneas paresque nobis
novem continuas fututiones*
—Gaius Valerius Catullus (84-54 BC)

Translation: "But stay at home and prepare for us nine acts of fucking, one after the other."

Bunk: Awe . . . **fuck.**
McNulty: **Motherfucker.**
Bunk: **Fuck. Fuck. Fuckin' fuck.**
McNulty: **Fuck.**
Bunk: Mmm, **fuck fuck** . . . **Fuck. Fuck. Fuck.**
McNulty: **Fuck?**
McNulty: **Fuck!**
McNulty: **Fuck.**
Bunk: **Mother-Fucker!**
McNulty: Awe **fuck** . . . Awe **fuck.**
McNulty: **Fuck, fuck, fuck, fuck** . . . **Fucker.**
McNulty: **Fuck, fuck, fuck, fuck.**
Bunk: Awe **fuck.**
Bunk: Mother **fucker.**
McNulty: **Fuckin-A.**
McNulty: **Fuuhck.**
McNulty: **Motherfucker.**
Bunk: **Fuck** Me.
—*The Wire*

fuck, n.

jerk; *American*

> Look up "pompous **fuck**" in the dictionary, and you'll find a picture of a DMV clerk next to it.

F Is for Film

Pulp Fiction. The Big Lebowski. Goodfellas. Boondock Saints. These classic movies (okay, well maybe not *Boondock Saints*) are all known for their colorful dialogue . . . but the grand prize winner goes to *Casino,* in which the F-word appears a record 422 times.

fuck buddy, n.

a person someone has sex with, but has no emotional obligation with as in a relationship; *American*

> For people who are congenitally incapable of long-term romantic relationships, being **fuck buddies** is a fun and commitment-free alternative.

Top Ten Fuck Buddies Wish List

1. Tina Fey
2. Jon Stewart
3. Drew Barrymore
4. Ryan Reynolds
5. Katherine Heigl
6. James Franco
7. Sandra Bullock
8. Will Ferrell
9. Amy Adams
10. Vince Vaughn

fuck like rabbits, v.

to have frequent sex; *American*

> I'm surprised that either one of them has time to go to work because they **fuck like rabbits**.

fuck off, v.

to tell someone to get lost or scram; *American*

> I told that loser boyfriend of mine to **fuck off** forever.

> I'm no one's lap dog, you can't put me on a leash, and that was the attitude of it, **fuck off**.
> —*Johnny Rotten*

fuck over, v.

to cheat or scam someone; *American*

> That judge really **fucked over** my ex in court. But I'm the one paying palimony.

fuck someone's brains out, v.

to have intense sex with someone; *American*

> She had me so hard, I **fucked her brains out** for hours.

fuck up, v.

to mess up, make a mistake; *American*

> We couldn't call our boss such a fuck-up if he didn't **fuck up** so often.

> Half of life is **fucking up**, the other half is dealing with it.
> —*Henry Rollins*

fuck you, v.

common curse meaning "damn you"; *American*

> **Fuck you** and the horse you rode in on—that's what the cowboys say.

> **Fuck you**, **fuck you**, **fuck you**, you're cool, and **fuck you**, I'm out!
> —*Half Baked*

fuckable, adj.

attractive enough to sleep with; *American*

> **Fuckable** is as **fuckable** does.

fuckface, n.
jerk; *American*

Get your hands off my ass, **fuckface**!

fucking, adj.
used as an intensifier; *American*

George Clooney is not just handsome, he's **fucking** gorgeous!

You can't say '**fuck**' in school, you **fucking** fat ass!
—*South Park*

fucking A, n.
short for "fucking awesome"; agreement; *American*

Fucking A, that was a smacking double overhead. Epic surf, dude!

fuckwit, n.
moron; variation of nitwit; *American*

Despite his good grades, Jeremy was still known by all his friends as a **fuckwit**.

Fuck and Shit as Synonyms... for Each Other
When you're sick of using expressions with *fuck*, try *shit*—it's nearly as versatile:

- Funny as shit
- Shit for brains
- You're hot shit
- A shitload of blah-blah
- When the shit hits the fan
- I shit you not
- A piece of shit
- Your shit don't stink
- He's a good shit
- Get your shit together
- Shoot the shit
- Up Shits Creek without a paddle
- Tough shit
- Shit out of luck

fuck-you money, n.

money that buys you enough freedom to do what you like; *American*

The best kind of financial windfall is **fuck-you money**.

The more money I earn, the less they can stop me. Where I come from, it's called **fuck-you money**, because I don't have to take an ounce of shit from anybody.
—*Michael Moore*

fudge packer, n.

someone who likes to fuck someone in the ass (usually referring to a gay male but not always); *American*

Doing it with a **fudge packer** can be really messy—not that there's anything wrong with that.

full house, n.

having more than one STD at a time; *American*

I may have won the strip poker game with a royal flush, but unbeknownst to everyone I was also sitting on a **full house**.

full of shit, adj.

completely made-up; lying; *American*

That perverse prevaricator Craig was so **full of shit** when he talked about having sex with all of those supermodels.

Hey, I'm not square. You're the one that's square. You're **full of shit**, man.
—*Taxi Driver*

funbags, n.

breasts; *American*

Female boxers tend to have the sexiest, muscular **funbags**.

funch, n.
quickie gay sex; *American*

> If you have the time around midday, want to meet me at the sauna for **funch**?

functional, adj.
homosexual; *American*

> After two years in prison, he became **functional**.

> **DERIVATION:** From "functional homosexual," meaning someone who engages in homosexual acts because of absence of heterosexual partners.

fungus, n.
disgusting person; *American*

> Jack was so high on mushrooms that he slept with a **fungus**.

fur pie, n.
vagina; *American*

> I'd like me a piece of **fur pie** for dessert, with lots of whipped cream.

furvert, n.
person who enjoys sexual activity with stuffed animals; *American*

> **Furverts** are a dime a dozen. What's really wacky are those apple pie-fucking *American Pie* fans.

futanari, n.

hentai (sexual anime) characters possessing both female attributes and penises; *American*

> I got a great deal on the latest **futanari** hentai when I was in Japan. It came free with the purchase of two pairs of soiled schoolgirl's underwear.

futzer, n.

one who wastes time on useless or pointless activities; *American*

> Uncle Shlomo is a classic **futzer**. He doesn't wake up until noon, then spends most of the day doing crossword puzzles and complaining about the price of rugelach.

> **DERIVATION:** This word likely comes from "fuck" and "putz," the Yiddish word for a lazy person.

fuzz, n.

vagina; *American*

> I like when he runs his fingers through my **fuzz**.

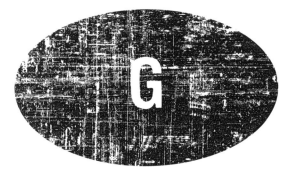

Gaelick, adj.
Irish sissy; *American*

On a month-long backpacking trip to the Emerald Isle, I discovered the sexy, brooding locals were actually a bunch of **Gaelicks**.

gagging, v.
begging; *American*

That dreamer Harold thinks every woman he meets is **gagging** for his dick.

DERIVATION: Gagging can also refer to the (involuntary) reaction that takes place when deep-throating a dick.

game show host, n.
guy who gets away with kissing women; *American*

David is a **game show host**. Me, I'm a slap magnet.

ABCDEF**G**HIJKLMNOPQRSTUVWXYZ

gang bang, n.

a sexual act where a group of people (three or more) have sex with one other person; *American*

> Initially the head cheerleader was the main attraction of the gang bangers, but lucky for her, the football team swung both ways—so when the so-called **gang bang** became a orgy of bisexual men, she escaped with her pompoms still intact.

> Okay, so what do you guys think this is, a **gang bang**?
> —*Grease*

Ganymede, n.

young gay male; *American*

> That **Ganymede** is a sweetheart, sure, but wait until he's legal, okay?

> **DERIVATION:** According to Greek mythology, Ganymede was kidnapped by Zeus, likely to perform sexual needs for the gods. The name actually means joy and intelligence, which is what sexual activity normally brings. . . .

gardening, v.

looking for sex outdoors or in a park; *American*

> The strangest thing is, my boyfriend says he's taken up **gardening** but even our cacti are dying.

gartersnake, n.

someone who's always trying to touch a woman's underwear; *American*

> Frank's such a **gartersnake** that I started going commando so he'd leave me alone.

gash, n.

vagina; *American*

> Gosh, what a filthy **gash**!

The Big Black Book of Very Dirty Words 147

gash for cash, n.
prostitution; *American*

> Alyssa has a tattoo on her thigh that says "**gash for cash**."

gay, adj.
homosexual; *American*

> Sure, my ex wasn't exactly a horndog, but I never suspected he was **gay**.

> David: You know how I know you're **gay**?
> Cal: How?
> David: Your dick tastes like shit.
> —*40 Year Old Virgin*

the gay cancer, n.
AIDS; *American*

> I'm sorry to have to be the one to tell you this, but Dad didn't die of a stroke . . . it was **the gay cancer**.

gay for pay, adj.
straight hustler who has sex with men for money; *American*

> When I hit rock bottom, it was **gay for pay** just to support my crack habit.

gaydar, n.
internal "radar" to identify homosexuals; *American*

> Sorry, boys, I'm straight—your **gaydar** is way off tonight.

gaylights, n.
highlights in a man's hair that may give off the impression he's gay; *American*

> Nice **gaylights**, Sonny, did your boyfriend do them for you?

gaylord, n.
homosexual; *British*

> Despite his tight pants and platinum hair, Roger is no **gaylord**.

> Despite his tight pants and platinum hair, Roger is no **homosexual**.

gayola, n.
money paid out to avoid anti-gay defamation; *American*

> Congressmen and Senators have paid out millions in **gayola** over the years to avoid being outed.

gazzing, v.
to orgasm; *American*

> Last night I heard my virgin neighbor finally **gazzing** with some nasty ho.

gearstick, n.
penis; *British*

> To help study for her driving test, Lisa practiced shifting her partner's **gearstick**.

> To help study for her driving test, Lisa practiced shifting her partner's **penis**.

geek rock, n.
cocaine; *American*

> In order to actually appreciate the Maroon Five concert, we had to score some **geek rock**.

geequals, adj.

two geeks who share the same level of trivial knowledge; *American*

My boyfriend is not exactly a *Star Wars* fan, but we're **geequals** on *Harry Potter*.

geezbag, n.

rude old person; *American*

Did you see the old guy who cut me off? What a **geezbag**!

gender bender, n.

transvestite; transexual; *American*

Boy George was the best of the British **gender benders**—I never knew whether to get a hard on or not when I watched his videos.

generic, n.

nameless sex partner; *American*

Then I slept with Phil, and then Dave, and then two **generics**.

GenQ, n.

generation queer; *American*

Is your sister **GenQ**? If not, can you give me her cell number?

gerbilling, v.

inserting gerbils in the anus for sexual pleasure; *American*

Urban legend has it that some homosexuals performed **gerbilling** in the 80s.

Brodie, how the hell else am I supposed to get the **gerbil** out?
—*Mallrats*

gerontophiliac, n.

person suffering from a sexual disorder involving attraction to the elderly; *American*

> I really hate my **gerontophiliac** history teacher—that sick fuck is totally into my grandma after she laughed at his lame jokes at open house.

get all up in that, v.

to sleep with someone; *American*

> I'm going to **get all up in that** if I play my cards right.

get it on, v.

to copulate; *American*

> Let's **get it on** while the getting's good, if you know what I mean.

get it up, v.

to have an erection; *American*

> It just figures that the one night I talk some drunken chick into coming home with me, I can't **get it up**.

get laid, v.

to have sexual intercourse; *American*

> Jesus if only I could **get** my mom **laid**, she'd get off my back about my grades.

> Oh, we are *so* gonna **get laid** tonight!
> —*Superbad*

get off, v.

to orgasm; *American*

> If I have a hard time **getting off** with just my hand, I just turn Mister Reliable up to full speed and let him do the dirty work.

get one's dick wet, v.
to have sex; *American*

> First date, and I **got my dick wet**. I see no reason for a second.

get one's pole varnished, v.
to receive a handjob; *American*

> My neighbor the gay antiques dealer loves restoring old furniture—second only to **getting his pole varnished**.

get stuffed, interj.
similar to fuck off, only not as harsh, meaning "no way!"; *British*

> You wanna watch *Strictly Come Dancing*? **Get stuffed**, I'm not watching that shite.

> You wanna watch *Dancing with the Stars*? **Fuck off**, I'm not watching that crap.

> Well I hope you told him to **get stuffed**.
> —*Casualty*

get together for cocktails, v.
women get together for drinks and sex talk; *American*

> Let's leave the boyfriends at home and **get together for cocktails**.

ghetto booty, n.
a big, firm butt; *American*

> If that girl's **ghetto booty** ran the world, there would be global peace.

> **Booty** is just a **ghetto** expression, and I'm just a **booty** star.
> —*Richard Pryor*

gift giver, n.
an HIV infected homosexual man who knowingly spreads his illness; *American*

> Christmas is a **gift giver's** favorite time of year—the bigger the package, the more it will be appreciated.

ginormous, adj.
extremely large; *American*

> Sorry Stan, but you're **ginormous**! There's no way you're putting that whole thing inside me.

DERIVATION: Ginormous is a compound term made up of the words giant and enormous.

> Hey! Have you seen these toilets? They're **ginormous**!
> —*Elf*

giraffe, n.
someone who enjoys eating ass; *American*

> His breath isn't bad for a **giraffe**.

the girls, n.
breasts; *American*

> Sorry I can't make the game tonight—I get to handle my wife's **girls** tonight and it so rarely happens.

give a shit, v.
to care about; *American*

> I'm sorry, I think that you've mistaken me for someone who **gives a shit**.

> Rehabilitated? It's just a bullshit word. So you go on and stamp your form, sonny, and stop wasting my time. Because to tell you the truth, I don't **give a shit**.
> —*The Shawshank Redemption*

give head, v.
to perform oral sex on a partner; *American*

> So, she wouldn't **give** Marcus **head** unless he talked like William Shatner while she did it.

give it up, v.
to copulate; *American*

> If Jessica doesn't **give it up** soon, I'll give up on her entirely.

> #1, I need a favor. #2, I didn't know we'd become such good friends. Because if we had, you'd know that I'd **give head** before I'd give favors and I don't even **give** my best friends **head**, so your chance of getting a favor are pretty slim.
> —*Go*

glamazon, n.
tall striking woman or drag queen; *American*

> Hot stuff! Is your **glamazon** packing a gun or a holster?

glass bottom boat, n.
a sexual act involving placing plastic wrap on someone's face before defecating on it; *American*

> Best birthday present ever? Had to have been that Caribbean cruise where I finally took my first ride in a **glass bottom boat**.

glass closet, n.
discrimination against homosexuals, preventing upward mobility in the workplace; *American*

> The glass ceiling is starting to chip away for gays, but unfortunately the **glass closet** isn't even scratched.

glaze the donut, v.

to ejaculate around an anus; *American*

> Bring your hot buns over here, baby, so I can **glaze the donut**.

GLIB, adj.

acronym for "good-looking in bed"; *American*

> My ex Sally was quite a natural beauty, and even after a sweaty night between the sheets, she sure was **GLIB**.

glory hole, n.

a hole in a men's bathroom stall in which a man sticks his penis through to be orally pleasured anonymously by someone on the other side; *American*

> What enquiring minds want to know: Was there a **glory hole** in that bathroom stall where Senator Larry Craig was allegedly caught making overtures to the undercover cop in the next stall?

go commando, v.

to not wear underwear; *American*

> Let's spice things up a little and **go commando**.

Actually, we're out of vests. But you can **go commando** if you want.
—*Navy NCIS*

go down, v.

to perform cunnilingus; *American*

> Be honest Jake, did you or did you not **go down** on Christine for Valentine's Day?

go to the boneyard, v.

to have sex; *American*

> No matter what stupid things Kevin says during dinner, it's our third date so I guess I'm **going to the boneyard**.

go to town, v.

to have sex with a partner; *American*

> If given the chance, I would absolutely **go to town** on that chick at the bar over there. And if pigs could fly, she'd let me.

> Look—my driver just pulled up. That's a sign. God wants us to leave here, get a good meal, and **go to town** on each other.
> —*30 Rock*

gobshite, n.

a person who talks nonsense; *British*

> I'll need more lager if I've got to sit with my brother-in-law Matt because he talks such **gobshite**.

> I'll need more beer if I've got to sit with my brother-in-law Matt because he talks such **shit**.

goddammit, interj.

to curse or condemn through heavenly intervention; *American*

> Watch out when the Colonel says, "**goddammit**." It means a five-mile march for all of us.

> I'm through being polite, **goddammit**! Now, take me down.
> —*Titanic*

going south, v.

to give oral sex; *American*

> I'm thinking of **going south** for a while; just don't come unless I tell you it's okay.

gokkun, n.

porn in which a person drinks semen; *American*

> Save the date—**gokkun** party at the club this Friday. Ladies drink free!

> **DERIVATION:** Gokkun comes from the Japanese onomatopoeia for gulp.

gold digger, n.

woman who searches out rich men for access to their money; *American*

> You can tell that **gold digger** mother of yours that since she's dating the mayor, she isn't getting a dime from me in child support this month.

golden shower, n.

a sexual act involving urination, generally a woman urinating on a man; *American*

> She told me her ex-boyfriend had a pee fetish and loved it when she gave him a **golden shower**.

Pee Is for Porn

Golden showers feature prominently in a number of films, most notably Barbet Schroeder's *Maitresse*.

gonads, n.

balls; *American*

> PT lost his **gonads** in a terrible hunting accident, but that has never stopped him from achieving his dream of felling a moose.

gonzo, n.
porn film with no plot, just sex; *American*

My girlfriend kept her arms crossed during the **gonzo** movie.

gonzos, n.
breasts; *American*

Gonzos, bongos, cantaloupes . . . I don't care what you call 'em, but they're all good words for a great thing.

gooch, n.
patch of skin between the balls and asshole; taint; *British*

Shut up or I'll wipe my sweaty **gooch** on your face

Shut up or I'll wipe my sweaty **taint** on your face.

goody trail, n.
trail of hair leading to genitals; *American*

Goody trails lead to either of two things, sweet treats or stanky leftovers.

goolies, n.
balls; *British*

Tea baggin' is dippin' your **goolies** in an obliging lady's mouth.

Tea bagging is dipping your **balls** in a horny lady's mouth.

God I love fishing. Well, obviously what I actually love is standing in cold water up to my **goolies**.
—*Chef!*

gooseberry, n.
third wheel; *British*

> I believe I ruined Peter's chances of scoring with Diana because I was the **gooseberry** on their date.

> I believe I ruined Peter's chances of scoring with Diana because I was the **third wheel** on their date.

gorb, v., n.
to eat hastily and greedily; a pig; *Irish*

> Did you see how that **gorb gorbed** a whole package of crisps?

> Did you see how that **pig gobbled** a whole package of potato chips?

gormless, adj.
clueless; *British*

> That chick was all over him but he was completely **gormless** until I pointed out that her hand was in his pants.

> That chick was all over him but he was completely **clueless** until I pointed out that her hand was in his pants.

Grand Canyon, n.
well-used, wide open anus; *American*

> There's just something so beautiful about visiting a woman's **Grand Canyon** for the first time.

grape smugglers, n.
speedos; *American*

> Poor Matt's dad is Italian and always wears his **grape smugglers** to the pool . . . how embarrassing.

grape squeezer, n.

a woman who can control her vaginal muscles; *American*

> You want to wear out your dick? That Monica is a **grape squeezer**.

grease the gash, v.

female masturbation; *American*

> The mechanic's wife couldn't understand why he spent all day with hot rods but she was left to **grease the gash** by herself.

greenhouse tan, n.

to be visibly naked in front of windows; *American*

> Natalie is working on her **greenhouse tan**.

greet-and-meat, n.

get together for sex; *American*

> You don't have time for a lot of emotional sharing at a **greet-and-meat**.

> **DERIVATION:** Pun on "meet-and-greet," which is when a person is presented to a crowd for quick introductions.

grizzle, v.

to gripe; *Scottish*

> My dad says Uncle John **grizzles** because my aunt won't stick a butt plug up her ass when they have sex—unless he will.

> My dad says Uncle John **complains** because my aunt won't stick a butt plug up her ass when they have sex—unless he will.

grope, v.

fondle sexually in a haphazard or clumsy fashion; *American*

> Micky the bartender **groped** my breasts, but it was mostly worth it because I got free drinks all night.

> **Groping** in a broom closet isn't dating. You don't call it a date until the guy spends money.
> —*Buffy the Vampire Slayer*

group grope, n.

a sexual act where a group of men masturbates together, or masturbates each other; *American*

> Screw making small talk with nasty chicks at the frat party tonight—who's in for a **group grope** instead?

grower not a shower, n.

a man whose flaccid penis appears quite small but becomes significantly larger when erect; *American*

> I wouldn't judge a book by its cover. Andrew looked small at the pool but he could be a **grower not a shower**.

growler, n.

a hairy vagina; *American*

> I saw my roommate's girlfriend naked by accident once a decade ago, and I still dream about her groovy **growler**.

grrl, n.

young feminist woman who is particularly aggressive about her beliefs; *American*

> **Grrls** don't just want to have fun anymore; they want to have equal fun.

grundle, n.

area between a man's anus and testicles; barse; *American*

> Don't be such a grump—go down on me and I'll suck you off while stroking your **grundle**.

G-spot, n.

short term for the Graffenberg Spot located inside the front wall or anterior of the vagina and very sensitive to arousal; *American*

> Pedro failed so many times at finding her **G-spot** that he would just give up and play video games, so he could win at something.

Top Five G-Spot Positions

1. Woman on Top
2. Doggy Style
3. Spooning
4. Woman on Top, Backwards
5. The Peacock

> What's the difference between a golf ball and a **G-spot**? I'll spend twenty minutes looking for a golf ball!
> —*In the Company of Men*

G-string, n.

a narrow piece of cloth designed to cover the pubic area held on by a string; *American*

> Inside every woman, there's a **G-string** stripper dying to get up on a pole and dance every once in a while.

> Molly, they're going to see a smiling snatch if you don't fix this **G-string**.
> —*Showgirls*

DERIVATION: The original "geestring" was the 1800s-era term used to describe the string that held up the loincloth worn by Native Americans. By the 1930s, G-string also referred to the underwear primarily worn by strippers at the time. Pinup girl Betty Page caused a sensation in the 1950s when she donned her own handcrafted G-strings. Times have changed.

guaranteed delivery, n.
definite sexual partner; *American*

> That chick at the pool table is a **guaranteed delivery**.

gully hole, n.
a vagina; *American*

> Chad's coming on to that brainiac, claiming that he likes smart women, but really he's only after her **gully hole**.

gumball machine, n.
a man who comes quickly; *American*

> Unfortunately, Harry is a real **gumball machine**. Of course, that gives me more time to read.
>
> **DERIVATION:** You stick it (the quarter) in, and out it (the gumball) comes.

guppie, n.
homosexual young urban professional; *American*

> **Guppies** have transformed San Francisco's Castro district into one of the liveliest neighborhoods in town.
>
> **DERIVATION:** Gay plus yuppie makes up the origin of this term.

gusher, n.
a woman who squirts when she comes; *American*

> We have to change the sheets every day. My girlfriend is a real **gusher**.

guy with a pie, n.

cross-dressing lesbian; pre-op female-to-male transsexual; *American*

My lesbian sister's ultimate pie in the sky would be a **guy with a pie**.

gymbot, n.

robot-like, workout-focused person at the gym; *American*

In every Gold's Gym there's a **gymbot** who doesn't like to be interrupted.

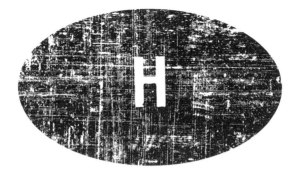

hag fag, n.
gay male who spends a lot of time with straight female friends; *American*

> **Hag fags** and fag hags make the ultimate best friends for women. Who doesn't love shopping and talking about men?

half a horse, n.
a man who's only hung half as well as a horse; *American*

> It's a good thing he's talented with his tongue because he's barely **half a horse**.

half and half, n.
session with a prostitute involving both oral and vaginal sex; *American*

> If you can afford it, a **half and half** is the best way to cream.

Halloween party, n.
an event that involves dressing up in costumes to engage in sexual fantasies; *American*

> I need to get a eye-patch for tonight's **Halloween party**.

to hammer, v.

to have hard penetrating sex; *American*

> Frank **hammered** me so hard last night that I can barely walk this morning.

---

handjob, n.

the sexual act of using one's hand to stimulate someone's penis; *American*

> Give me a **handjob** for a bit first, and then we can either screw or you can blow me until I'm good and hard.

---

handlebars, n.

a pig-tail hairstyle; *American*

> Men really go for that naughty schoolgirl thing, so Rhonda always wears **handlebars** when she's out on campus trolling for profs.

---

handwarmers, n.

breasts; *American*

> Sweetie, if you've lost your gloves, just come over here and I'll put my **handwarmers** to work for you.

---

hanky panky, n.

sex; *American*

> When you're serious about doing the **hanky panky**, you're not on the dance floor any more.

I don't think so. First of all, there will be no holding hands. There will be no looks across the room. There will be no touchy-feely, there will be no **hanky-panky**, there will be no smoochy-woochy. And there will be none of that other stuff you're not supposed to know about.
—*Roseanne*

happy ending, n.
a handjob received after a massage; *American*

> The massage is great, and then the **happy ending** tops it off.

happy shopper, n.
bisexual; *American*

> A **happy shopper** never has to go home without a purchase.

DERIVATION: From the fact that a bisexual has twice the choice.

> So, Nurse Gandhi-rella, I need you to suction this guy, do a wet-to-dry dressing change, and, oh, what the hell, go ahead and top him off with one of your special, special sponge baths. **Happy ending** optional—his choice, not yours.
> —*Scrubs*

happy trail, n.
trail of hair leading to the genitals; *American*

> Don't shave your **happy trail** . . . it helps me feel my way to your dick in the dark.

happy valley, n.
cleft between the buttocks; *American*

> Happiness is waking up in a **happy valley**.

hard swap, n.
allowing your partner to have sex with someone not in your presence; *American*

> We're trying something different, a **hard swap**.

hard-on, n.
erect penis; *American*

> Ronald took too many Viagra and ended up with the **hard-on** from hell.

> When a naked man is chasing a woman through an alley with a butcher's knife and a **hard-on**, I figure he isn't out collecting for the Red Cross!
> —*Dirty Harry*

hardwood floors, n.
shaved genitals and anus; *American*

> After polishing my knob, I paid the hustler to lick my **hardwood floors** clean.

Harry Johnson, n.
penis; *American*

> My **Harry Johnson** and I go way back—he's been my right hand man since middle school.

Harvard style, n.
masturbation between another man's lubricated thighs; *American*

> What we did is not gay, it's **Harvard style**.

hasbian, n.
former lesbian; *American*

> That's what we commonly refer to as a "**hasbian**."
> —*The L Word*

> Let's face it, you're nothing but a **hasbian**—the minute you started dressing like an MTV tramp and subscribing to *Cosmo*, I knew our relationship wouldn't last.

have a party, v.

to have sex; *American*

> Want to come over and **have a party**? There'll be plenty of booze involved.

have honey in the hips, v.

to be a smooth lover with noticeable experience; *American*

> Tyrone is such a magnificent lover; I'd swear he **has honey in the hips**.

have sexual intercourse, v.

to copulate; *American*

> Foreplay is fine for an appetizer, but **intercourse** is the hungry man's meal.

Synonyms for Intercourse:

attack the pink fortress	copulate	get some nooky
ball	dance with	get some stanky
bash the beaver	do the funky chicken	giggity giggity
be intimate with	do the horizontal bop	go at it
beat	do the hunka chunka	go to bed with
beat cakes	do the laundry	grease
beat cheeks	do the nasty	GTD
boff	dog	hang some curtains
boing	dukin'	have relations with
boink	fire	have sex
break one off	fluff	hide the German sausage
breed	fornicate	hide the salami
BUFU	freakin'	hit it
bump nasties	frequent	hit skins
bunce	fubb	hizzit the skizzins
bury the weasel	geit	hump
chop up	get guts	jazz
clap	get some booty	kertang
consummate	get some dippings	kick it ›››

Synonyms for Intercourse—continued

kill it	ride dick	skronk
knock it out	ride the flagpole	slay
lay pipe	ride the skin bus to	sleep with
lie with	tuna town	spank
make happy happy	roll in the hay	squeak
make sexy time	run train	stang
piece of ass	scuff	swag
pile	serve	tap ass
poonj	shaboink	whoo hoo
rail	skrog	

headfuck, n.

someone who messes with someone's mind; *American*

> That crazy **headfuck** first cockteased me, then attempted to do the same to my friend who right away told her to fuck off.

headlights, n.

breasts; *American*

> Check out the **headlights** on that sweet Corvette over there. If she needs a tune-up my drill is good and ready.

he-blow, n.

homosexual Jewish male; *American*

> I've had it with **he-blows** and their guilt; I'm going exclusively goy from now on.

heifer, n.

a fat woman; *American*

Harriet is such a **heifer**.

I feel like such a **heifer**. I had two bowls of Special K, 3 pieces of turkey bacon, a handful of popcorn, 5 peanut butter M&M's and like 3 pieces of licorice.
—*Clueless*

helicoptering, v.

rotating a penis in someone's face; *American*

Helicoptering was cool when I was like, twelve, but I wouldn't wave my dick around a girl's face now unless it was going in her mouth.

hen night, n.

bachelorette party; *British*

For Tiffany's **hen night**, the girls hired a stripper who looked like Carrot Top, so it ended up being a very short party.

For Tiffany's **bachelorette party**, the girls hired a stripper who looked like Carrot Top, so it ended up being a very short party.

hen-pecked, adj.

being ordered around by a woman; pussy-whipped; *British*

Henry is so **hen-pecked**—he literally left his own bachelor party because his fiancée called and told him to leave.

A husband is a man who when someone tells him he is **hen-pecked**, answers, yes, but I am **pecked** by a good hen.
—*Gill Karlsen*

Henry is so **pussy-whipped**—he literally left his own bachelor party because his fiancée called and told him to leave.

hentai, n.

Japanese animé featuring graphic sex; *Japanese*

For horny cartoon buffs, a late-night **hentai** takes the cake.

hermaphrodite, n.

person born with both male and female sex organs; *American*

Hermaphrodite porn is my favorite, but sadly there aren't many of them to enjoy.

Wait a minute, we heard that rumor in my high school! You were the **hermaphrodite** cheerleader from Long Island?
—*Friends*

DERIVATION: This term comes from the Greek gods Aphrodite and Hermes. As the story goes, they had a child, the immortal Hermaphroditus, who was transformed into an androgynous being when a nymph's wish that they were never separated was granted by the gods.

hessian, n.

male prostitute; *American*

Of course he's friendly, he's a **Hessian**.

DERIVATION: This term comes from mercenaries hired by Britain to fight the American colonists.

heteroflexible, adj., n.

straight man who occasionally has sex with other men; *American*

My fiancé is not gay! He's **heteroflexible** but I don't mind. It saves me from ever having to go anal.

hide the salami, v.

to copulate; *American*

Next time you want to play **hide the salami**, the butcher's daughter is a real hottie.

You wanna play "**hide the salami**" with his old lady?
—*The French Connection*

hierophilia, n.

sexual fetish involving religious objects; theophilia; *American*

> I think I'm into **hierophilia** . . . our young Irish priest is hot, but I would be more into some action with the cross itself.

high heels, n.

sex position with the female lying down facing the male with her legs around his waist or alternately on his shoulders; *American*

> If your lover is lacking in the size department, try **high heels** for deeper penetration.

high maintenance, n.

a person who takes a lot of money and time to make happy; *American*

> That woman with all the Mr. T bling is way too **high maintenance** for my hippie buddy Sam.

> You're the worst kind [of woman]; you're **high maintenance** but you think you're low maintenance.
> —*When Harry Met Sally*

himbo, n.

male bimbo; *American*

> Jimbo the **himbo** packs a mean nine inches but couldn't read a book to save his life.

> He lusted after me, but I had to spurn his advances, because he's a **himbo**.
> —*I Think I Do*

hirsutophilia, n.

sexual attraction to body hair; *American*

> Too bad I've got such a **hirsutophilia** problem. I'd totally be into banging Stephen Colbert, but I have a sneaky feeling he's bald as an eagle down there.

hit that, v.

to have sexual intercourse; *American*

> She is way out of your league . . . you couldn't **hit that** with a ten foot dick if you tried.

hitching post, n.

penis; *American*

> The best way to get hitched is to grab him by the **hitching post**.

hold someone like a bowling ball, v.

to insert two fingers into a woman's vagina and one in her anus; *American*

> He may have been a champion at the alley, but Ivan's attempts to **hold his wife like a bowling ball** did not go over well.

holy week, n.

when a woman is menstruating; *American*

> If you're horny, Father, we'd better get a round in tonight—next week is **holy week**, and not even you are allowed in my place of worship.

home movies, n.

amateur sex films; *American*

> We spent the weekend shooting **home movies**.

home-cooked biscuits, n.

lover or lovemaking skills one returns to in the end for satisfying but familiar sex; *American*

> He may not be the best lay around, but when I'm craving baby gravy, Johnny's **home-cooked biscuits** do just fine.

honeydew, n.
a demanding partner; *American*

> His honey is a **honeydew**.

> **DERIVATION:** From the phrase, "honey do this."

honkers, n.
breasts; *American*

> With double-d **honkers** and a caboose to match, my first love will always have a special place in my . . . umm . . . heart.

hook up, v.
to meet for sex; *American*

> Jill and I first **hooked up** in the bathroom at TGI Fridays.

hooker, n.
a prostitute; *American*

> My friend once asked me if he should tip his **hooker**, and I told him, "If she has all her teeth and you don't catch anything from her, I don't see why not."

Coach: You getting a lot of satisfaction from those 15 dollar **hookers**?
Chazz: I am *never* satisfied! It's a curse.
—*Blades of Glory*

Hooray Henry, n.
brainless, rich, upper-class man; *British*

> Common thieves are more respectable than the **Hooray Henry** of the London Stock Exchange.

> Common thieves are more respectable than the **brainless greed mongers** of Wall Street.

hooters, n.
breasts; *American*

Nicole may not have much between her ears, but those **hooters** of hers make up for it.

hoover, n.
an amazing blowjob; *American*

She gave me such a **hoover** I thought my eyes were going to implode.

DERIVATION: Some think this term is derived from the Hoover brand vacuum for its amazing sucking ability.

Old Mc Bundy had a farm, B-U-N-D-Y. And on this farm there was no wife, B-U-N-D-Y. With-a no wife here and a-no kids there. A hooker coming over on Friday nights. With big luscious **hooters**, a pizza, and a beer there. Old Mc Bundy had a farm, B-U-N-D-Y.
—*Married with Children*

horizontal refreshment, n.
sexual intercourse; *American*

At the play's intermission, we left the theater for a little **horizontal refreshment** behind the dumpsters.

horrify the children, v.
to engage in acts that would horrify a child walking into the room; *American*

After spending the whole evening at the circus, maybe tonight we can risk **horrifying the children**?

hot beef injector, n.
penis; *American*

My ex is a vegetarian but she sure loved a **hot beef injection** now and again.

hot dogging, v.
to have sex; *American*

> Since listening to his last album, I am plagued by nightmares that Snoop Dogg is **hot dogging** me in my bathroom.

hot pocket, n.
the act of defecating inside a pullout couch then shutting it so the next guest who uses it will be alarmed by the shit; *American*

> Ralph is always passing out at my house so I decided to leave a **hot pocket** for him in the couch, but when he discovered my shit, he just shrugged and passed out next to it.

hotbox, n.
a closed area where marijuana smoke can't escape and fills up the vehicle or room; *American*

> After a while of being in the **hotbox**, we had some serious munchies. So we stopped off at a donut shop and gracefully stepped out of the car, smoke following us, in front of some cops.

hotdog, n.
penis; *American*

> When you're the **hotdog** for her roll, that's some kind of picnic.

ABCDEFG**H**IJKLMNOPQRSTUVWXYZ

Hugh, n.

an older man who surrounds himself
with young women; *American*

> My grandfather is such a **Hugh**. He
> dumped my grandma after forty years
> of marriage and took up with his
> twenty-five-year-old nurse.
>
> **DERIVATION:** From Hugh Hefner of
> *Playboy* fame.

Playing Hard to Get

Hugh Hefner is perhaps the world's
most famous bachelor. He has admitted to sleeping with thousands of
women, notably the Playmates who
grace the cover of his magazine,
Playboy.

hummer, n.

a blowjob; *American*

> My dream is to get a **hummer** in a Hummer.

hump 'em and dump 'em, v.

to sleep around; *American*

> Tony's a real **hump-'em-and-dump-'em** kind of guy.

hump the dump, v.

to have anal sex; *American*

> My wife is such a sweetheart—she never says no to **humping the dump**.

hung like a hamster, adj.

possessing a small penis; *American*

> He may have been **hung like a hamster**, but the
> veterinarian had a sweet side the ladies couldn't resist.

hung like a horse, adj.

to have a huge dick; *American*

> They may say size doesn't matter, but if you're **hung like a horse**, then you know better.

> You guys like Conan? He's **hung like a horse**, you know. A horse named My Little Pony!
> —*Late Night with Conan O'Brien*

hustler, n.

male prostitute; *American*

> Tell that **hustler** to fuck off; I'm no queer.

hybristophilia, n.

sexual attraction to criminals; *American*

> We used to just call it the "Bonnie and Clyde syndrome" but now there's a fancy name for it—**hybristophilia**.

hypersexual, adj., n.

someone obsessed with sex; *American*

> My **hypersexual** wife demands sex every night and I just can't keep up with her.

hypoxyphilia, n.

sexual disorder involving reduced oxygen supply to the brain to induce pleasure; *American*

> Believe it or not, there are an estimated 2 million deaths per year due to **hypoxyphilia**, also known as sexual asphyxiation.

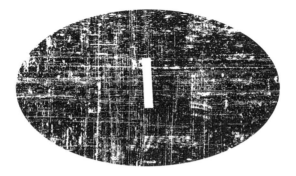

ice cream sandwich, n.

one white woman between two black men; *American*

> The only thing better than an **ice cream sandwich** is watching one behind a two-way mirror while you jerk off.

in the doghouse, adj.

in trouble; *American*

> When her impotent boyfriend found used condoms in the trash, Sarah was **in the doghouse**.

> Well, if it isn't Xena's little bitch! Welcome to **the doghouse**!
> —*Xena: Warrior Princess*

inchworm, n.

small penis; *American*

> My first time was oddly painless—I thank my lucky stars it was an **inchworm** that broke me in.

indoor plumbing, n.

man with a vagina; *American*

> It turns out that Felix has **indoor plumbing**, if you know what I mean.

infantilism, n.

sexual fetish with infant role play; *American*

> She's willing to put me in a diaper, spank my ass, and hold me like a baby? Where do I sign up? **Infantilism** hotties don't get any better than that.

in-law sex, n.

quiet sex; *American*

> I almost bit off Alex's hand during **in-law sex** when he tried to keep me from screaming.

> Sex at the in-laws or while the in-laws are over is a rarely admitted to but frequent act.

intercorpse, v.

to have sex with someone who isn't responsive; *American*

> I get tired of the monthly **intercorpse** with my wife, and as a result, the local hookers know me by name.

Internet beauty, n.

someone who exaggerates their charms online; *American*

> My blind date was an **Internet beauty**; she definitely wasn't the size six she had claimed to be.

intersexual, adj.

hermaphrodite; *American*

> Jamie Lee Curtis? No matter what the rumors, I don't believe she's **intersexual** for a minute.

This is my Peter—uh, my "friend" Peter. We just met at the, uh, **intersexual** . . . homosection . . . INTERSECTION!
—*In & Out*

Irish kisses, n.
the act of farting on someone's face; *American*

> Harry's girlfriend would often give him **Irish kisses** if he didn't wake up after the alarm clock went off.

Irish mutton, n.
syphilis; *American*

> Visit any Boston-area bar for a belly warming helping of **Irish mutton**.

Irish toothache, n.
pregnancy; *Canadian*

> Caitlin went to the dentist to have a root canal and didn't take it well when he said she looked like she had an **Irish toothache**. Caitlin wasn't pregnant.

> Caitlin went to the dentist to have a root canal and didn't take it well when he said she looked like she was **pregnant**. Caitlin wasn't pregnant.

Irish twins, n.
siblings born less than a year apart; *American*

> **Irish twins**: the result of too much Guinness and too little intelligence.

it, n.
vagina; *American*

> I'm hitting **it** tonight, even if I have to make a booty call.

Italian hanger, n.

a sexual position where the woman lies on her back and the man holds up her legs and feet during intercourse; *American*

> Ralph's flexible girlfriend finally talked him into doing yoga after she introduced him to the **Italian hanger**.

Italian necktie, n.

the act of slicing a person's throat and pulling his or her tongue out through the wound; *American*

> The Naples mafia, known locally as the Camorra, specializes in **Italian neckties**.

Italian Stallion, n.

an attractive Italian man who has a large penis; *American*

> Stella's boyfriend, Anthony, might seem like an **Italian Stallion**, but he doesn't actually know how to use his equipment to her satisfaction.

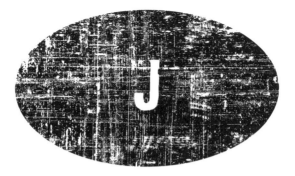

jackal, n.
a guy who will sleep with anyone; *American*

> Why would you ever agree to date Mike? He's such a **jackal**.

to jackhammer, v.
to have sexual intercourse; *American*

> I only date construction workers. They don't make much money, but they do know how to **jackhammer**.

> Definitely a **jackhammer**. I'm in there with some pressure, and when I'm done you're not the same as before. You're changed.
> —*Mallrats*

jack-in-the-box, n.
penis; *American*

> Trevor got me the sweetest gift for my birthday 'cause he knows I love beef—a handmade gift certificate to his **jack-in-the-box**.

jailbait, n.
underage girls; *American*

> Hey, those biddies might want our junk but they are definitely **jailbait**.

jam, adj.
gay slang for a straight male; *American*

> Amanda's new boyfriend may be hot, but let's not forget, guys, he's just a **jam**, okay?

> **DERIVATION:** Jam stands for "just a man."

---

jam sandwich, n.
police car; *British*

> Is that a **jam sandwich** behind us because only the bill could tailgate us that closely?

> Is that a **police car** behind us because only a cop could tailgate us that closely?

---

janitor, n.
someone who agrees to take out the least attractive person; *American*

> Tom is such a **janitor** that he must be shortsighted.

> Tom so often **picks up the homeliest** girls that he must be shortsighted.

> **DERIVATION:** A janitor is known as someone who takes out the trash.

---

jawbreaker, n.
giant cock; *American*

> Some good advice: Never bite a **jawbreaker**, let it slowly melt in your mouth.

---

jello shot, n.
jello made with vodka and set in a shot glass; *American*

> Three **jello shots** later and I couldn't feel my legs.

Jeremy, n.
a skanky male; *American*

> I wouldn't fuck Todd for all the money in the world. He's such a **Jeremy**.

> **DERIVATION:** From the celebrated porn star Ron Jeremy.

More to These 9.75 Inches than Meets the Eye

You may know him only as the top adult male porn star of all time, but Ronald Jeremy Hyatt started his career as a special education teacher. Besides holding a Masters degree, "the Hedgehog" also holds the record for porn performances, with more than 2,000 films to his credit.

jerkin' the gherkin, v.
male masturbation; *American*

> Brad was late to class because he was **jerkin' the gherkin**.

> Problem now is every time we **jerk the gherkin**, we end up with a lot of unwanted, sticky white stuff everywhere, right?
> —*Weeds*

jiffy pop, n.
orgasm; *American*

> Thirty minutes of sucking his dick, one minute of sex, and bam, **jiffy pop**.

jilt, v.
to receive an orgasm without giving one; *American*

> After he **jilted** me again, I reached for my battery-powered Mister Reliable.

jism, n.
semen; *American*

> **Jism**, despite what your boyfriend may insist, is not one of the four food groups.

jizz, v.

to ejaculate; *American*

> Well, excuse me if it helps me **jizz** when a girl dresses up like a naughty schoolgirl.

> Then I want you to fuckin' flick my nuts while your friend spanks me off in the same Dixie cup that Silent Bob **jizzed** in.
> —*Jay & Silent Bob Strike Back*

jizz whistle, n.

penis; *American*

> At band camp, I learned to play the skin flute and the **jizz whistle**.

John Thomas, n.

penis; *American*

> When he told her his penis went by the name **John Thomas**, and could she please call it that, she laughed out loud.

John Lover

"John Thomas" was immortalized in *Lady Chatterley's Lover* by D.H. Lawrence. Originally banned for obscenity in Britain, the novel was published in Italy in 1928.

Johnson, n.

dick; *American*

> He whipped out his **Johnson** on the bus, but all he really had to do was pull on the chain to make the bus stop.

> Don't you just want to feel that cozy little box grip down on your **Johnson**?
> —*Sideways*

DERIVATION: "Johnson" owes its name to early twentieth century boxer Jack A. Johnson, the first African American to win the world heavyweight championship. When racist white America assumed he had a big penis because he was black, thereby accounting for his sexual prowess with white women, he allegedly stuffed his pants to good effect.

join at the groin, v.
to fuck; *American*

Here's some candy and flowers. Now let's **join at the groin**.

jugs, n.
breasts; *American*

Only jugheads are into **jugs**. I'm a leg man myself.

Great! That'll give me time to get my **jugs** waxed.
—*Blades of Glory*

juice the moose, v.
to fart; *American*

Dude, you better roll down your window because I'm about to **juice the moose**.

jump start, v.
to do whatever it takes to get someone in the mood for loving; *American*

For our first weekend away together, I **jumpstarted** the journey with flowers and champagne.

junk, n.
penis; *American*

My **junk** would fit into her DSL quite nicely.

junk in the trunk, n.
a nice large ass; *American*

That dancing chick with the **junk in the trunk** at the club mesmerized every dude in the place with that sweet swinging ass.

Aha! A little **junk in the trunk**, it's a Finch slam dunk.
—*Just Shoot Me*

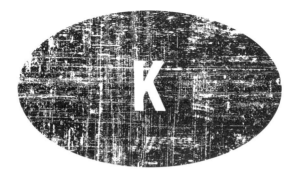

kangaroo, v.
to place the penis in a vagina and not move; *American*

> Why don't you just **kangaroo** for a while until I moisten up a bit?

keptie, n.
mistress; *American*

> The French woman in 2B is 3A's **keptie**.
>
> **DERIVATION:** Keptie comes directly from "a kept woman."

key party, n.
a party where housekeys are put in a bowl to decide who goes home with whom; *American*

> Last weekend I went to a **key party** and went home with a stranger.

kick the tires, v.
to try someone out before committing; *American*

> I'm going to **kick the tires** before I start getting serious.
>
> **DERIVATION:** From kicking the tires before buying a used car.

kickin', adj.

smelly; malodorous; *American*

> In the five weeks since his girlfriend moved out, Sam went from well-groomed to **kickin'**—and his apartment wasn't much better.

kickstand, n.

penis; *American*

> The Olympic gymnast could suck her coach's **kickstand** while doing a handstand . . . now that's impressive.

killographic, adj.

containing violent content; *American*

> The wildly popular *Grand Theft Auto* is one of the most **killographic** video games ever to win the hearts and minds (and some would say souls) of every fourteen-year-old boy.

> **DERIVATION:** The expression killographic was created as a label for "graphic depiction of brutal violence" by the National Institute of Media and the Family.

kindergarten math, adj.

easy; *American*

> Talk to the trampy girl at the bar, she's **kindergarten math**.

kinky, adj.

weird, in a sexual context; *American*

Kinky is in the eye of the beholder.

DERIVATION: The word "kink," meaning a "twist in a rope," dates back to the 1670s. Not until 1959 was the word "kinky" used to refer to sexual acts.

The best kind of **kinky** sex is to have **kinky** sex with your wife or husband, the person you love.
—*Frank Langella*

---

kiss the lips that never speak, v.

to perform cunnilingus; *American*

For a special Valentine's Day treat, I'm going home to **kiss the lips that never speak**.

---

kissing fish, n.

lesbians; *American*

If you're looking for same-sex love you might try the bar down the street—Tuesday is **kissing fish** night.

---

kiwis, n.

testicles; *American*

If you shave so I don't spit up a hairball afterward, I'd gladly suck your **kiwis** while fondling your shaft.

---

klismaphiliac, n.

person who derives pleasure from enemas; *American*

John Kellogg, of Kellogg's cereal fame, believed in enema "cures" and is considered a classic example of **klismaphiliac** behavior.

knee trembler, n.

hurried sex while standing; *British*

I had a **knee trembler** with her in the toilet, while her bloke was at the bar.

We had a **standing quickie** in the bathroom stall, while her boyfriend was at the bar.

The Peacock's Knees

In the Kama Sutra, lovers are advised to "feed the peacock" in a standing sex position designed for passion in a hurry.

knob, n.

penis; *American*

To open the door, turn the knob. To open the man, suck the **knob**.

knob-end, n.

dick head; *British*

My **knob-end** is tender after last night's escapades.

My **dick head** is sore after last night's action.

knock boots, v.

to have sexual intercourse; *American*

Last night I went home with a sexy go–go dancer and we **knocked boots** until the sun came up.

knocked up, adj.

pregnant; *American*

I should have wrapped it up because now she's **knocked up** and expects me to be a responsible father. I think I'll move to Ireland instead.

By the way, who **knocked up** the journalist?
—*The Life Aquatic with Steve Zissou*

knockers, n.
breasts; *American*

> Valentina was a real knockout—**knockers** and all.

. . . .

know someone in the biblical sense; v.
to have had sexual intercourse with someone; *American*

> I **knew my high school boyfriend in the biblical sense**, but we only did it while his parents were at church on Sundays.

. . . .

Kringle, n.
the act of waking up a partner for sex; *American*

> You'd have bags under your eyes too if you'd been **Kringled**.

> **DERIVATION:** From Kris Kringle, Santa Claus, who comes down the chimney in the middle of the night.

kumquat, n.
a total sexpot; *American*

> I stood at attention when I caught sight of that Thai **kumquat**.

> **DERIVATION:** Besides being a delicious Asian fruit, kumquat is a cumulative pun on cum and twat.

KY Jelly, n.
sex lubricant; *American*

> **KY Jelly** is the grease that makes the sex machine go round and round.

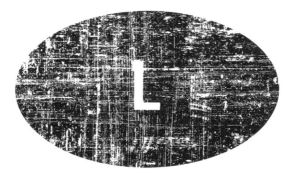

lactoids, n.
breasts; *American*

> Jenna's **lactoids** were seriously engorged the entire six months she was milking.

ladder, n.
run (in tights or pantyhose); *British*

> Oi, you look like a right slapper with that big **ladder** in your stockings.

> Whoa, you look like a real slut with that big **run** in your stockings.

lady-bazzers, n.
tits; *British*

> I often motor boat her **lady-bazzers** until I pass out from exhaustion.

> I often motor boat her **tits** until I pass out from exhaustion.

lairy bloke, n.

man who ogles women, dirty old man; *British*

> The shuffleball court is always full of **lairy blokes**.

> The shuffleball court is always full of **dirty old men**.

lashed, adj.

drunk; *British*

> After failing my A-levels, I got **lashed** to forget my worries, or at least pass out.

> After flunking my exams, I got **drunk** to forget my worries, or at least pass out.

leather cheerio, n.

anus; *American*

> Twenty years of daily ass-fucking and Quentin's **leather cheerio** was tough as nails.

leathered, adj.

drunk; *British*

> You should've seen us at karaoke last night, we were absolutely **leathered**.

> You should've seen us at karaoke last night, we were absolutely **hammered**.

leg man, n.

a man who gets turned on by a woman's legs; *American*

> The longer the legs, the harder Sean's dick. He's a real **leg man**.

legless, adj.

really drunk; *British*

> I didn't think someone could get so **legless** on champagne, but Denise is truly a lush.

> I didn't think someone could get so **smashed** on champagne, but Denise is truly a lush.

lemon party, n.

three or more old, fat, gay men with flaccid penises in an orgy; *American*

> Everybody loves a **lemon party**—or not.

lemon tart, n.

blonde slut; *American*

> That girl is nothing but a **lemon tart**.

lemonade, n.

semen or sometimes urine; *American*

> How about some **lemonade** to quench your thirst?

lemons, n.

breasts; testicles; *American*

> When life gives you **lemons**, well, you had better just thank God for his generosity.

let one go, v.

to fart; *American*

> Whoever **let that one go** must've indulged in the musical fruit burrito last night.

lick the jar clean, v.

to lick someone's anus; *American*

> I **like to lick the jar clean**, but only when it's really dirty.

lick-suck, n.

fellatio; *American*

> Please, I'm not asking for an hour-long blowjob, sweetie, just a quick **lick-suck**.

licorice stick, n.

penis; *American*

> I love **licorice sticks**—as long as it's good and plenty.

light in the loafers, adj.

gay; *American*

> Gavin's constant talk of bedding random women was clearly a front for being **light in the loafers**.

Limey, n.

a Brit; *British*

Sydney's full of **Limeys** these days. It's a disaster—from some Aussies' point of view.

Sydney's full of **Brits** these days. It's a disaster—from some Aussies' point of view.

DERIVATION: The term Limey comes from British sailors' use of lime juice to prevent scurvy.

Two **Limey** fucking filmmakers hanging from their skinny pricks over an 8th floor balcony, for shooting unauthorized footage of an Arty Cohen fighter. This! This is my definition of a situation!
—*The Calcium Kid*

limpwristed, adj.

homosexual; *American*

Colonel Peters? I haven't asked and he's not telling, but I wouldn't be surprised if that **limpwristed** old queen enjoyed his time in the trenches.

Wonder how he'd react if his son had a **limp wrist** with a pulse.
—*Heathers*

lingerie, n.

undergarments worn by a woman to arouse her partner; *American*

I was aroused by my wife's **lingerie,** but then wondered how much it cost; this thought decreased my arousal.

I wear women's leggings under my clothes, but no **lingerie**.
—*Dennis Rodman*

link the pink, v.

to have sex; *American*

After a romantic dinner and a few glasses of wine, we're going to **link the pink**.

lip crispies, n. ·

cold sores; oral herpes; *American*

> Sorry boys, no blowjobs tonight—
> I've got a screaming case of the
> **lip crispies**.

lipstick lesbian, n.

a lesbian who is feminine and
attracted to other feminine lesbians;
American

> When actress Anne Heche was going out with mega-celeb Ellen DeGeneres,
> the media dubbed her the most famous **lipstick lesbian** in the world.

> Oh! I see. I guess man
> whores should have to
> drink from a separate water
> fountain. Actually, that's
> probably a pretty good idea.
> Might have a case of the
> "**lip crispies**."
> —*The Colbert Report*

liptease, n.

the act of putting on lipstick in a sexually suggestive
way; *American*

> A well-performed **liptease** can prove as effective a strategy
> as its counterpart, the striptease.

lizzing, v.

laughing and peeing at the same time;
American

> Don't make me laugh too hard—after
> three kids, I risk **lizzing** with each joke.

> I'm **Lizzing**!
> —*30 Rock*

DERIVATION: Coined by Tina Fey of *Saturday Night Live* fame, lizzing is a
combination of the word laughing and the slang term whizzing, for urinating.

lob, v.

to cause a woman to look up so you can stare at her breasts; *American*

> The only reason Will learned about constellations was so he could **lob**.
>
> **DERIVATION:** From a lob in tennis where someone hits the ball so that it makes a high arc.

---

lobster, n.

man who likes to pinch women; *American*

> After learning that Nate was a **lobster**, I never stood too close to him.

---

lock crotches, v.

to have sexual intercourse; *American*

> First we locked lips, then we **locked crotches**.

---

locust, n.

an over-eager lover; *American*

> Pam discovered that ice water was an effective tool to use on her **locust** boyfriend.

---

lollipop stop, n.

truck stop where there are prostitutes or hustlers; *American*

> The highlight of our coast-to-coast roadtrip was the **lollipop stops** every ten miles.

---

lollypop, v.

to perform oral sex on a man; *American*

> Heather got so horny watching porn that all she could think of was **lollypopping** her boyfriend when he came home from work.

London Bridge, n.

the act of two guys having sex with two girls from behind while the girls are facing each other on all fours and making out; *American*

> Many things have to go well for a **London Bridge** to become a reality . . . many more things for it to work. Thinking of the logistics involved gives a whole new meaning to **London Bridge** is falling down.

look both ways, v.

to check out someone's breasts; *American*

> Remember to always **look both ways**, especially when a hottie crosses the street.
>
> **DERIVATION:** From the advice: look to the left and the right before crossing the street.

lookism, n.

discrimination based on physical appearance; *American*

> It's **lookism** all right—Clyde may have a great personality and make lots of money, but I still wouldn't do him without a bag over his head, or mine.

loose change, n.

someone you use when you don't have any other options; *American*

> After spending all evening with a tease, I checked for any **loose change**.

lose the plot, v.

to go crazy; *British*

> Mark **lost the plot** after he caught his brother shagging his wife.

> Mark **went crazy** after he caught his brother fucking his wife.

---

loser, n.

a good-for-nothing or unsuccessful person; *American*

> He's thirty, unemployed and still living with his parents? Ditch the **loser**.

---

lot lizard, n.

a prostitute working truck stops; *American*

> Cindy was a real **lot lizard**, banging all the truckers that stopped for a hot meal.

---

love muscle, n.

penis; *American*

> Manuel pictured the Governator's throbbing **love muscle** every night while jerking off.

---

love shack, n.

a place where one goes to have sex; *American*

> Claudia's parents were home, so this weekend her parents' room couldn't double as a **love shack** for all her friends.

Mac: Wow, so that's the saddest thing I've ever heard. You guys are **losers**. Dennis: How are we **losers**, dude? Mac: Well, maybe it boils down to this, smart guy: computers are for **losers**. Dennis: And you're drinking a beer at 8 o'clock in the morning. Mac: Whatever, dude, irrelevant.
—*It's Always Sunny in Philadelphia*

love wand, n.

penis; *American*

> Check out my **love wand**—want to see my magic in action?

lube the tube, n.

anal sex; *American*

> Break out the booze and **lube the tube**.

lucky Pierre, n.

third invitee to sex with a gay couple; *American*

> My first night in Paris, I had the good fortune to be a **lucky Pierre** to a sexy duo of French queens.

LUG, n.

female college student who sleeps with women while in school; *American*

Don't fall in love, she's just a **LUG**.

DERIVATION: LUG stands for "lesbian until graduation," which is a term that many current "straight" women must admit applied to them.

Top Ten Hottest Lesbians of all Time

1. Sappho
2. Portia de Rossi
3. Jodie Foster
4. Ellen
5. Joan Baez
6. Melissa Etheridge
7. Queen Latifah
8. Rosie O'Donnell
9. Eleanor Roosevelt
10. Amelia Earhart

luggage, n.

a woman who's a sex object; *American*

> At midnight, Henry showed up at the hotel with some old **luggage**.
>
> **DERIVATION:** From a woman being nothing but a box (pussy) and bags (breasts).

lunch meat, n.

mid-day sex; *American*

> Jess is some serious **lunch meat**.

lungs, n.

breasts; *American*

> They might be fat and the music might be horrible, but you have to admit that most female opera singers have a nice set of **lungs**.

luppie, n.

lesbian young urban professional; *American*

> Lucky for you, you found a **luppie** who lives in a fabulous apartment . . . I'm still stuck with Nancy in her one-room studio, barely making ends meet.

lush, n.

a person who gets drunk easily and is, in most cases, flirtatious; *American*

> The difference between **lush** and lust is just one martini.

Dean (Martin) was sometimes redundant: both his arrangements and his drink situation were **lush**, man.
—*Sammy Davis Jr.*

lust, n., v.

the attraction or desire to have someone; to desire to have sex with someone based on physical attraction; *American*

> I had a deep **lust** for the bartender, but when I found out she really enjoyed *Battlestar Galactica*, I fell in love with her.

What am I saying? If I poached this beast's lower horn, am I any better than that ranger with his demented foot **lust**? Yes. But not by enough.
—*Futurama*

....

LXIX, n.

69; *American*

> When in Rome, **LXIX**.

DERIVATION: In Roman numerals, LXIX is 69. Pronounced "lexis."

macaroni and cheese, n.

$5 bag of marijuana and dime bag of cocaine; *American*

> Dinnertime kids! It's spaghetti and meatballs for you and **macaroni and cheese** for mommy and daddy.

to mack on someone, v.

to hit on, flirt with someone; *American*

> That hooker was **mackin' on my husband** so I popped her one.

> Ronald McDonald proved to be a huge flirt with all the women at the clown retirement home. In fact, they called him the Big **Mack**.
> —*Dame Edna*

mack-daddy, n.

a man who goes out with a lot of women, and has a lot of dates; *American*

> Danny got three numbers at the party tonight—what a **mack-daddy**!

mad, adj.
crazy; *British, American*

That was a **mad** party last night—I don't even know how I ended up waking up on the back porch with a dog licking my face.

That was a **crazy** party last night—I don't even know how I ended up waking up on the back porch with a dog licking my face.

Anybody remotely interesting is **mad**, *in some way or another.*
—*Doctor Who*

madam's apple, n.
bulging Adam's apple on a woman; *American*

Look at that lady with the mustache and the **madam's apple**. Gross!

Madame Palm and her five daughters, n.
masturbation; *British*

It's **Madame Palm and her five daughters** for me again tonight because I ran out of money for whores. It's a tough economy.

It's **masturbation** for me again tonight because I ran out of money for whores. It's a tough economy.

magic wand, n.
penis; *American*

David Copperfield is the only magician I'd let near me with his **magic wand**.

mainlining, n.
injecting illegal drugs directly into one's veins; *American*

By the time he finished sixth grade, Dennis had gone from smoking a little weed to **mainlining** heroin.

make a sexy time, v.

to have sexual intercourse; *American*

C'mon baby, you wanna go **make a sexy time** with me in the toilets?

DERIVATION: This expression, as well as several other sexual terms that have entered our recent vocabulary, comes from Sacha Baron Cohen's Borat character.

Look, there is a woman in a car! Can we follow her and maybe **make a sexy time** with her?
—*Borat: Cultural Learnings of America for Make Benefit Glorious Nation of Kazakhstan*

make babies, v.

to copulate with the intent of procreation; *American*

Enough with the pull-out method—let's **make babies** instead.

make love, v.

to copulate; *American*

No offense, but I never said I wanted to **make love** to you, just plain old fuck you.

make out, v.

to kiss progressing to the level of touching; *American*

I shouldn't have **made out** with my boss at the Christmas party. Must have been a case of the beer goggles.

make whoopee, v.

to have sexual intercourse;
American

> Vanessa and I **made whoopee**
> on her parents' bed and spent
> half an hour trying to get the cum
> stains out before they got home
> from the movies.

Brandi: Second suitor: if we
were **making whoopee**, what
sounds would you make?
Brodie: Wait, what's **whoopee**?
Brandi: You know, being
intimate.
Brodie: What? Like fucking?
—*Mallrats*

maki roll, n.

the piece of skin left over after a
dog or cat is neutered; *American*

> Rex rolled over on his back in bed and, when I turned around, his **maki roll**
> was right in my face.

making an omelet, v.

a sexual act that involves ejaculating in a woman's ear,
and folding it over; *American*

> I decided to be an asshole, so I came in her right ear and
> folded it over, thus, **making an omelet**. I am awesome.

mamma jamma, n.

something or someone very sexy; *American*

> Garth's new English Lit professor is such a bad **mamma jamma**—he's
> actually reading Chaucer in the original Middle English.

man boobs, n.

enlarged breasts on a man; *American*

> I'd do Patrick if he didn't have those awful fatty **man boobs**.

> I quite like the idea of getting fat, growing a pair of **man boobs** and going bald, sitting in a big mansion eating cake with the kids running about.
> —*Danny Dyer*

man cave, n.

a place where men can hang out without being bothered by a girlfriend or wife; *American*

> Adam built himself an amazing **man cave** in the basement complete with a pool table, bar, and big-screen TV. He went down there three weeks ago and hasn't been seen since.

man pit, n.

promiscuous woman's bedroom; *American*

> Watch out. Sophie will slip you a mickey and drag you back to her **man pit** if you're not careful.

mangina, n.

a vagina-like shape, formed when a man tucks his penis and balls between his legs then puts them together; a gay man's anus; an emasculating insult; *American*

> If, after a rough night of anal action, your mangina is cracked or bleeding, try sitting on an ice cube to dull the pain.

DERIVATION: Man plus vagina equals mangina.

> Brennan has a **mangina**!
> —*Step Brothers*

manny, n.
male nanny; *American*

> These days all the cool celebrities want **mannies**, not nannies.

Top Five Hollywood Mannies

1. Robin Williams in *Mrs. Doubtfire*
2. Tony Danza in *Who's the Boss*
3. Sebastian French in *Family Affair*
4. Hulk Hogan in *Mr. Nanny*
5. Scott Baio in *Charles in Charge*

manor, n.
neck of the woods; hood; *British*

> I know the way—it's my **manor**.

> I know the way—it's my **hood**.

manscape, v.
to shave a man's body hair, esp. pubic hair; *American*

> My girlfriend likes it when I shave my balls, so I **manscaped** last night.

mantsy, adj.
extremely horny; *British*

> Oooh, David Beckham's big bulge makes me positively **mantsy**.

> Oooh, David Beckham's big bulge makes me positively **horny**.

manwich, n.
a threesome between two men and one woman; from man + sandwich; *American*

> Yum, I'd love to be the meat in a Snoop Dogg/Flava Flav **manwich**.

marital aid, n.
sex toy; *American*

> Sex with my wife just isn't what it used to be; I say we give **marital aids** a try as a last ditch effort before I start banging hookers on business trips.

Mary Jane, n.
marijuana; *American*

> Roll a spliff and let's smoke some **Mary Jane**, dude.

Maserati, n.
crack pipe made from a plastic bottle and rubber spark plug; *American*

> The broker lost it all in the crash of '89 and traded his Ferrari for a **Maserati**.

master of one's domain, n.
a person who can go without masturbating for long periods of time; *American*

> *Seinfeld* aside, I've never understood why one would aspire to be the **master of one's domain**.

masturbate, v.

to stimulate one's sex organs to the point of orgasm; *American*

When you can't be with the one you love, **masturbate**.

Hey, don't knock **masturbation**— it's sex with someone I love.
—*Annie Hall*

DERIVATION: While there is no certain derivation for masturbate, many believe that it comes from the Latin words *manus* meaning "hand" and *turbare* meaning "to create chaos." Which seems about right.

Synonyms for Masturbate:

Assault on a friendly weapon	Dishonorable discharge
Backstroke roulette	Disseminating
Baiting your hook	Do the dew
Batting practice	Doddle whacking
Being your own best friend	Doodle your noodle
Bludgeon the beefsteak	Drain the vein
Boppin' your bologna	Dropping a line
Box the Jesuit (sixteenth-seventeenth century!)	Dropping stomach pancakes
Buffing the banana	Fist your mister
Burping the worm	Five against one
Butter your corn	Five-finger knuckle shuffle
Calling all cum	Flute solo
Calling down for more mayo	Freeing the Willies
Carrying weight	Frigging the love muscle (British)
Changing your oil	Getting in touch with your manhood
Charm the cobra	Getting in touch with yourself
Choke the sheriff and wait for the posse to Come	Getting to know yourself personally in the "biblical sense"
Clean the pipes	Giving it a tug
Clean your rifle	Greasing your bone
Clubbing Eddy	Hack the hog
Couch hockey for one	Hand to gland combat
Crank the shank	Hands-on training
Crown the king	Have one off the wrist
Custer's last stand	Having a Roy (Australian)
Date Miss Michigan	Hitchhike under the big top
Date Mother Palm and her five daughters	Holding all the cards
Devil's handshake (Catholic school)	Holding your sausage hostage
Diddle	Hone your bone
	Hump your fist ›››

Synonyms for Masturbate (continued)

Hump your hose
Humpin' air
Ironing some wrinkles
Jack hammer
Jack off
Jackin' the beanstalk
J Arthur Rank
Jelly roll
Jenny McCarthy jaunt
Jerk off
Jiggle the jewelry
Jimmying your Joey
Knuckle shuffle on your piss pump
Launching the hand shuttle
Making nut butter
Making yogurt
Mangle the midget
Manipulate the mango
Manual override
Masonic secret self-handshake
Massage your muscle
Massage your purple-headed warrior
Measuring for condoms
Meeting with Palmala Handerson
Milking the lizard
Milkywaying
Molding hot plastic
Nerk your throbber
Oil the glove
One-handed clapping
One-man show
One-man tug-o-war
Paddle the pickle
Pam Anderson polka
Pat the Robertson
Peel some chilis
Play pocket pool
Play the organ
Play the piss pipe
Play the pisser
Play the skin flute

Play the stand-up organ
Playing with Dick
Playing with Susi Palmer and her five friends
Playing with the snake
Playing your instrument
Plunk your twanger
Pocket pinball
Pocket pool
Polish the chrome dome
Polish the rocket
Polish the sword
Pounding your pud
Pud wrestling
Puddin'
Pudwhacking
Pull the root
Pull your taffy
Pulling the wire
Pulling your goalie
Pump the python
Pumping for pleasure
Punchin' the clown
Punchin' the munchkin
Punishing Percy
Punishing the bishop
Ride the great white knuckler
Rolling the fleshy blunt
Roman helmet rumba
Ropin' the longhorn
Roughing up the suspect
Rounding up the tadpoles
Runka (Swedish)
Scratching the itch
Seasonin' your meat
Sending out the troops
Shake the snake
Shaking hands with Abe Lincoln
Shaking hands with shorty
Shaking hands with the governor
Shifting gears
Shooting Sherman ›››

Synonyms for Masturbate (continued)

Shucking Bubba
Slammin' the salami
Slap boxing the one-eyed champ
Slap my happy sacks
Slappin' Pappy
Slapping the clown
Slapping the cyclops
Slinging jelly
Sloppy Joe's last stand
Sloppy sign language
Stroke the stallion
Smacking your sister
Spank your monkey
Spear chucking
Spreading the mayo
Spunk the monk
Squeeze the cream from the flesh Twinkie
Squeeze the lemon
Squeezing the tube of toothpaste
Squeezing the burrito
Staff meeting
Stall clapping
Stroke off
Stroking it
Stroking your goat
Stroke your poker
Taking a shake break
Tame the wild hog
Tap the turkey
Tease the python
Tease the weasle
Tenderize the meat
The erky jerk
The sticky page Rumba
Threading a needle
Throw off a batch
Throwin' down
Thump the pump
Tickle the Elmo
Tickle the pickle
Toss off

Toss the boss
Toss the turkey
Tugging your tapioca tube
Tugging your tubsteak/tubesnake
Tug of war with cyclops
Tuning the antenna
Turning Japanese (UK—one step beyond wanking)
Tussle with your muscle
Unwapping the pepperoni
Varnishing the cane
Wailing
Walk the dog
Walking Willie the one-eyed wonder worm
Wank (British)
Wax your Jackson
Waxing the dolphin
Whipping the one-eyed wonder weasle
Whipping the pony
Whipping the window washer
White-water wristing
Whizzin' jizzim
Wiggling your worm
Winding the Jack-in-the-box
Wonk your conker
Working a cramp out of your muscle
Working your Willy
Wrestling the eel
Wring out your rope
Wring your thing
Yahtzee
Yank my doodle (it's a dandy)
Yank off
Yank the yodle
Yank your crank

*Reprinted with permission from *WTF? College*, Adams Media, 2009.

matchbox, n.

half a dozen marijuana cigarettes; *American*

> Hey kid, hands off my **matchbox**—you're too young to take more than just a few hits.

matressable, adj.

fuckable; *American*

> Claire might not be supermodel material, but she's definitely **matressable**.

MBA, n.

Married but available; *American*

> Like I said, there are far too many middle-aged **MBAs** who think they're hot shit at work these days.

McJob, n.

crappy job, often in the food service industry; *American*

> Now that the global recession's hit, I'll be lucky to find anything but a **McJob**, if that.

McJobs for Everyone

One in ten Americans have worked at McDonald's, according to CBS News.

meals on wheels, n.

attractive bicyclist; *American*

> San Francisco's steep hills ensure the buns of local **meals on wheels** delivery boys are hard enough to eat a meal off of.

meat popsicle, n.
dick; *American*

> When it's hot in the summer and I'm dripping with swan sauce, only a **meat popsicle** will do.

meatspace, n.
reality, as opposed to virtual reality; *American*

> On Facebook, Meat Loaf and I are friends, but back here in **meatspace** I go to bed alone.

medallion man, n.
man going through a midlife crisis; *British*

> My dad has become a real **medallion man**. He wears a gold chain, drives a Jaguar, and tries to flirt with every pussy under twenty-five he comes across.

melolagnia, n.
sexual arousal derived from music; *American*

> When Tara, who suffers from **melolagnia**, first heard Beethoven's Ninth Symphony, she had an incredible urge to play the skin flute.

ménage à trois, n.
sexual activity involving three people; *French*

> My ultimate fantasy is a **ménage à trois** with Britney Spears and Lindsay Lohan.

> My ultimate fantasy is a **threesome** with Britney Spears and Lindsay Lohan.

When in France . . .

This term literally means "three-person household" in French, and implies that the three are one big couple. So unless you want to move in with your threesome partners, don't use it in France! To simply imply that you'd like to have sex with two other people at the same time, use the expression, *faire l'amour à trois,* to make love with three, instead. This way you're guaranteed a good time on a Saturday night, but spared of the annoyance of not only one girlfriend or boyfriend, but two!

menglish, n.

coded language used by men that is incomprehensible to women; *American*

Don't bother trying to decipher what men are saying. **Menglish** is second only to Chinese in difficulty. Wait a second, there's Chinese menglish as well!

merkin, n.

pubic wig; *American*

Kate Winslet has been quoted as saying that she was asked to wear a **merkin** during the sex scenes in *The Reader*, but declined. No wonder she won an Oscar for that role.

DERIVATION: The word merkin probably comes from the English *malkin*, meaning mop.

The Merry Merkin

Women started wearing merkins back in the 1400s—some because they'd shaved their pubic hair to prevent pubic lice, and others to hide the symptoms of venereal disease.

merry-go-round, n.

one person sleeps with another, then that person sleep with another, and the cycle continues; *American*

My office is a regular **merry-go-round**. Just yesterday we found out the boss had slept with the receptionist, who slept with the head accountant, who in turn screwed the boss.

meshuga, adj.

crazy; *American*

Divorce your husband, the doctor, for a plumber? Are you **meshuga**?!?

DERIVATION: Meshuga is the Yiddish word for crazy.

metrosexual, n.
a well-groomed urban male who dresses stylishly and draws comparisons to homosexuals; *American*

> My boss isn't gay; he just likes his accessories to match his outfit— a typical **metrosexual**.

microrgasm, n.
a small, quiet, short orgasm that lacks satisfaction; *American*

> If Juan got a **microrgasm** out of his high maintenance girlfriend, he felt like it was at least a small triumph; of course, he did tell his friends that he had her screaming all night long.

miffed, adj.
fed up; *American*

> Christine was so **miffed** with her husband's bad behavior that she refused sex for a week.

mighty mouth, n.
someone who gives a good blowjob; *American*

> Not sure if I regret breaking up with Eve or not. On one hand, she could be a real bitch, but on the other hand, she was a **mighty mouth**.

> **DERIVATION:** This term is a play on the cartoon character Mighty Mouse.

MILF, n.

acronymm for "Mother I'd Like (to) Fuck"; *American*

Check out the juicy ass on Tanya's mom. She's a **MILF**.

milkshake, n.

body; *American*

Tyra's **milkshake** is damn sexy—look at that big booty!

DERIVATION: The term milkshake was first heard in the Kelis song of the same name. The simplistic song features few lyrics, all of which focus on whose milkshake is the best. Despite this fact, the single was a hit worldwide, reaching number three in the U.S. and number two in the United Kingdom, in addition to being in the top ten in the Netherlands, Belgium, Sweden, and New Zealand.

Millennium Falcon, n.

a person who one is embarrassed to have had sexual intercourse with; *American*

Wanda thought she had bagged a hottie at the *Star Wars* convention, but when during sex her Chewbacca-portraying date finally removed his mask, she asked that **Millennium Falcon** to put it back on.

Millennium Falcon was the name of Han Solo's spaceship in *Star Wars*. And yes, any normal person who has gone to bed with a *Star Wars* fan after one too many beers can proudly say they've taken a ride in a Millennium Falcon as well.

mimbo, n.

male bimbo; *American*

That hot surfer is a real **mimbo**: Body by Nautilus, brains by Mattel.

DERIVATION: This term was popularized in "The Stall" episode of *Seinfeld*.

minder, n.
bodyguard, security guard; *British*

> You should've seen the size of Beckham's **minder**—he could have kicked my ass worse than his employer.

> You should've seen the size of Beckham's **bodyguard**—he could have kicked my ass worse than his employer.

mini-me, n.
a smaller or younger lookalike; *American*

> If my kid sister doesn't take off my boots immediately, I'll wallop that bratty little **mini-me**.

> **Mini-Me**, stop humping the "laser." Honest to God! Why don't you and the giant "laser" get a fricken room for God's sakes?
> —*Austin Powers: The Spy Who Shagged Me*

minty, adj.
gay; *American*

> Don't go with the green sweater—people will think you're **minty**.

missile launcher, n.
penis; *American*

> If Don't Ask Don't Tell is repealed, I'll sign my **missile launcher** up for active duty, stat.

Mister Reliable, n.
vibrator; dildo; *American*

> When your lover disappoints, turn to **Mister Reliable.** He never fails to please.

Moaning Minnie, n.
whiner; *British*

> Don't be such a **Moaning Minnie** and wingman for me so I get that fit bird.

> Don't be such a **whiner** and wingman for me so I get that sexy biddy.

mofo, n.
motherfucker; *American*

> I'll show that badass **mofo** who's boss.

mojo, n.
charisma; ability to attract a partner; *American*

> When he lost his job at the bank, Curtis lost both his money and his **mojo**.

mollycoddled, v.
to be babied; *British*

> No wonder Will is immature—his mother has **mollycoddled** him all his life and I wouldn't be surprised if he has some serious Oedipus complex.

> No wonder Will is immature—his mother has **babied** him all his life and I wouldn't be surprised if he has some serious Oedipus complex.

> To me, I didn't join the forces to be **mollycoddled** or treated any differently. As far as I am concerned, in my eyes, if Harry can do it, then I can do it. I want to fight in Afghanistan.
> —*Prince William*

money shot, n.
moment of orgasm in a porn movie; *American*

> Oh, that's right, baby, open your mouth, it's time for the **money shot**.

moobs, n.
man boobs; *American*

> Victor thought chicks were jealous of his massive **moobs**, and never second-guessed himself.

moose, n.
dog; *British*

> Clara may be a **moose**, but she does have nice baps.

> Clara may be a **dog**, but she does have nice tits.

mooseknuckle, n.
protruding genitalia on a man or woman; camel toe; *American*

> Check out that **mooseknuckle** at the bar . . . that guy either has a huge cock or way-too-small jeans.

motherfucker, n.
a terrible or contemptible person; a jerk; *American*

> Tell that **motherfucker** to bring back my bike that he stole or I'll call the police!

Yippee-ki-yay, **motherfucker**.
—*Die Hard*

motor boat, v.

placing one's face between giant breasts, shaking one's face, and blowing out; *American*

> I **motor boated** her until I passed out from joy and loss of breath.

mouth mattress, n.

someone who gives oral sex easily; *American*

> You remember that waitress whose number I got at the diner? I took her out for a pizza, and damn if that **mouth mattress** didn't make my night.

muff, n.

female pubic area; *American*

> Isn't that cute, she's shaved her **muff** into a heart for Valentine's Day.
>
> **DERIVATION:** The word muff comes from the Old French *moufle,* meaning "mitten."

muff diving, n.

cunnilingus; *American*

> The latest entry on newly married Brian's "Honey, Do" list: **muff diving**.

muffin top, n.

fat roll hanging over the waistband of a person's too-tight jeans; *American*

> If only Tania would buy her jeans another size up, she could avoid that nasty **muffin top**.

mug, n.
easy to fool person; *British*

> Strangely, even though she's wearing that stupid hat with the feathers, she's not a **mug**.

> Strangely, even though she's wearing that stupid hat with the feathers, she's not a **fool**.

muggle, n.
inferior or unskilled person; *British*

> See that **muggle** in the corner of the pub drooling over a pint? That's my brother.

> See that **inferior person** in the corner of the bar drooling over a pint? That's my brother.

> Clearly. Associating with **muggles**. And I thought your family could sink no lower.
> —*Harry Potter and the Chamber of Secrets*

DERIVATION: Muggle is a term created by JK Rowling, author of the Harry Potter series. Originally, it referred to a person lacking in magical powers but has now come to mean any idiot.

municipal cockwash, n.
promiscuous woman; *American*

> Even if she were the last woman on earth, I'd rather my dick shrivel up and fall off than give it a go in that **municipal cockwash**.

mutt's nuts, adj.
fantastic; *British*

> Sally's eyes are still the **mutt's nuts**, even when she wears too much eyeliner.

> Sally's eyes are still **fantastic**, even when she wears too much eyeliner.

....

mysophilia, n.
sexual disorder involving dirty or soiled items, usually underwear; *American*

> When my wife accidentally shit her pants, me being the **mysophiliac** I am, I thought I'd die of a hard-on.

> **DERIVATION:** This term comes from the Greek *mysos*, meaning "uncleanliness," plus *philia*, meaning "an affinity for."

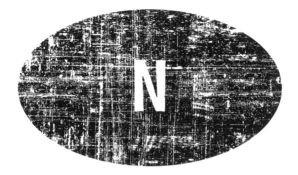

naff, adj.

lame, crap; in poor taste; *British*

> A girl who gets uppity and rude about a guy opening the door for her is **naff**, so you should let it slam in her face.

> A girl who gets uppity and rude about a guy opening the door for her is **lame**, so you should let it slam in her face.

nancy/nancy boy, n.

pathetic person; homosexual; *British*

> Don't be such a **nancy** and get in the ocean; you've got a wetsuit on!

> Don't be such a **pathetic person** and get in the ocean; you've got a wetsuit on!

Stop being such a little **nancy boy**.
—*Epic Movie*

to narc, v.

to inform on someone; *American*

> When he got so stoned he missed school, Roger's little brother **narced** him out to his parents and he got grounded for a month. He'll never give his little brother any weed again.

If you're going to kick me out, kick me out. Don't make me look like a **narc** to my friends.
—*Toy Soldiers*

narked, adj.
pissed off; *British*

> When Ewan got dumped for merely looking at another chick's ass, he was really **narked**.

> When Ewan got dumped for merely looking at another chick's ass, he was really **pissed off**.

narratophilia, n.
sexual arousal from dirty talk; *American*

> Don't forget to pick up a copy of *The Big Black Book of Very Dirty Words* for your favorite **narratophiliac** today.

nasty, adj.
cool; *American*

> *Grand Theft Auto* is the **nastiest** game; my little brother plays it night and day.

necrophilia, n.
the act of having sexual intercourse with a human corpse; *American*

> If someone has sex with a zombie, technically that person is into **necrophilia**, and has way too many issues to solve in a lifetime of therapy.

nerdling, v.

to baby or coddle an inexperienced or naïve person, especially one who shows anti-social or overly technical behavior; *American*

> Stop **nerdling** your son and just take away his video games once and for all.

new lad, n.

modern young man who is sophisticated and thoughtful; *British*

> I want a **new lad** like Gwen's husband. He picks up around the house and even changes the baby's nappies.

> I want a **modern man** like Gwen's husband. He picks up around the house and even changes the baby's diapers.

newcummer, n.

gay man new to the homosexual scene; *American*

> Sure, I can introduce you to that guy over there, but be warned, he's a **newcummer**.

to nick, v.

to steal; *British*

> You really shouldn't **nick** that dog—nobody on this planet would pay money for that unruly creature.

> You really shouldn't **steal** that dog—nobody on this planet would pay money for that unruly creature.

nickel bag, n.

five dollar bag of marijuana; *American*

> I've only got three bucks—will you go in with me for a **nickel bag**?

---

nimrod, n.

moron; *American*

> I couldn't believe Sarah married that **nimrod**, even if he was hung like a horse.

> Jules, if you give that fuckin' **nimrod** fifteen hundred dollars, I'm gonna shoot him on general principles.
> —*Pulp Fiction*

---

nipple clamps, n.

small, attachable clamps used to stimulate the nipples; *American*

> When Jamie got her nipples pierced, she started putting her **nipple clamps** on her husband instead.

---

no fats, femmes, or flamers, interj.

no overweight, overly feminine, or flamboyant gays; *American*

> A century ago it was "No Irish need apply"; now it's "**No fats, femmes, or flamers**."

> **DERIVATION:** This is a common line in gay classifieds, which limits the searcher's choice to "manly" men, or discreet gay men who act straight.

---

nonce, n.

pedophile; *British*

> Did you see the old geezer in that banger? He's definitely a **nonce** and nobody should ever accept candy from him.

> Did you see the old guy in that car? He's definitely a **pedophile** and nobody should ever accept candy from him.

noodle, n.
penis; *American*

> Chinese **noodles** are always a disappointment—and usually an hour afterward you're in the mood for something more substantial.

nooner, n.
brief sexual encounter, quickie; *American*

> I live ten minutes from work, and let me tell you, the best perk is an occasional **nooner**.

nose candy, n.
cocaine; *American*

> For Easter, my boyfriend skipped the traditional chocolate bunny and got me a gram of **nose candy** instead.

> Bill: So what're you doing babysitting stiffs? What were you ... drinker? Big drinker?
> Chuck: No!
> Bill: Doper! Toothead! **Nose candy**! Coke!
> —*Night Shift*

not batting with a full wicket, v.
not playing with a full deck, crazy; *British*

> Rob should never be your wingman because he's **not playing with a full wicket**, and might say something really insulting to your romantic interest.

> Rob should never be your wingman because he's **not playing with a full deck**, and might say something really insulting to your romantic interest.

to not give a toss, v.
to not give a shit; *British*

> Sorry, but I **don't give a toss** what you got for your birthday.

> Sorry, but I **don't give a shit** what you got for your birthday.

not the sharpest tool in the box, adj.
unintelligent, stupid; *British*

> I met my new boss today, and let's just say he's **not the sharpest tool in the box**.

> I met my new boss today, and let's just say he's **stupid**.

numbnuts, n.
idiot; *American*

> Hey **numbnuts**, get your fucking car out of my parking spot!

nunya, adv.
none of your business; *American*

> My wife kept asking too many questions, so I said, "You know what? **Nunya**!"

nut hangers, n.
really tight pants, mostly jeans, worn by guys; *American*

> I really hope that hipster with the **nut hangers** loses circulation and falls over so he can serve as a warning to all of those other kids.

to nut someone, v.
to head butt someone; *British*

> Do that again and I'll **nut** ya like I'm Zinedine Zidane in a football match.

> Do that again and I'll **head butt** ya like I'm Zinedine Zidane in a soccer game.

nuts, n.
testicles; *American*

> It makes Thomas' wife nuts when he scratches his **nuts** in public.

> Come on. Let's see some bananas and **nuts**. Oh, perhaps we should just pull their pants off.
> —*Arrested Development*

nutsack, n.
scrotum; *American*

> If you want her to suck your balls, you'd better shave your **nutsack**.

nutter, n.
mentally deranged person; *British*

> That half-naked dude who was walking down the middle of the street and talking to himself was a real **nutter**.

> That half-naked dude who was walking down the middle of the street and rapping to himself was a real **mentally deranged person**.

nyataimori, n.

the practice of serving sushi or sashimi off a naked woman's body; *Japanese*

> I'm headed to Japan for two weeks vacation. The top three things on my to-do list are to buy used schoolgirls underwear, rub up against people in the metro, and eat dinner at a **nyataimori** restaurant.

> I'm headed to Japan for two weeks vacation. The top three things on my to-do list are to buy used schoolgirls underwear, rub up against people in the metro, and eat dinner at a restaurant where they **serve sushi off of naked ladies**.

---

nympho, n.

woman obsessed with sex; short for nymphomaniac; *American*

> I told that **nympho** to get her hands off my ass but she wouldn't listen.

A **nymphomaniac** is a woman as obsessed with sex as the average man.
—*Mignon McLaughlin*

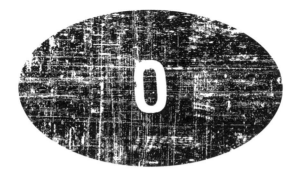

O face, n.

the face made when having an orgasm; *American*

> Have you ever seen an old Ron Jeremy porno? What a homely **O face**!

Obama, adj.

London street slang for cool; *British*

> You got dumped with a text? That is so not **Obama**.

> You got dumped with a text? That is so not **cool**.

I'm thinking I might take that new chick from Logistics. If things go well I might be showing her my **O-face**. "Oh . . . oh . . . oh!" You know what I'm talkin' about. "Oh!"
—*Office Space*

oculophilia, n.

sexual fetish involving the eye; *American*

> My last optometrist appointment was absolutely bizarre; as he examined my eyes, he licked his lips and I noticed that **ocuphiliac** had a giant hard-on.

off one's trolley, adj.
fucked up; out of one's mind; *British*

> You should've seen me at the bar last night—I was **off my fucking trolley**.

> You should've seen me at the bar last night—I was **fucked up**.

off the twig, adj.
dead; *British*

> Somebody come quick! My budgerigar is **off the twig**!

> Somebody come quick! My parakeet is **dead**!

> **DERIVATION:** This is a reference to the famous *Monty Python* "dead parrot" skit.

offer someone out, v.
to challenge someone to fight; *British*

> I'd had enough of him telling me how much he wanted my sister, so I **offered him out**. I don't actually have a sister, but it's the principle of the matter.

> I'd had enough of him telling me how much he wanted my sister, so I **challenged him to a fight**. I don't actually have a sister, but it's the principle of the matter.

Oi, interj.
meaning "hey"; *British*

> **Oi**, you shouldn't knock fucking someone in a graveyard until you've tried it!

> **Hey**, you shouldn't knock fucking someone in a graveyard until you've tried it!

old chap, n.
penis; *British*

> My **old chap**'s covered in warts, which isn't a good sign.

> My **penis**'s covered in warts, which isn't a good sign.

> It started long and thin, but someone has shredded this noble **old chap** on a mandolin.
> —*Stefan Gates, UK Times Online*, describing a Beijing restaurant that specializes in varieties of animal penises for consumption.

old navy, n.
heroin; *American*

> **Old navy** might be old-school, but for cheap shit it can't be beat.

the old slap and tickle, n.
sex; *British*

> No, your friend can't have **the old slap and tickle** with my mother while you watch!

> No, your friend can't have **sex** with my mother while you watch!

olfactophilia, n.
sexual arousal derived from smells; *American*

> Too bad I don't suffer from **olfactophilia**, otherwise there is no way I'd eat out your stanky, old cunt.

on the bricks, adj.
walking the streets looking for drugs; *American*

> Have you seen my roommate? Judging by the empty baggies on his bed I think he's **on the bricks**.

on the rag, adj.

menstruating; *American*

> I was about to go down on her, but she told me she was **on the rag**, so I fell asleep defeated.

one bomb, n.

100 rocks of crack cocaine; *American*

> Dear Santa: Forget the toys and bring me a **one bomb** this year.

one-eyed snake, n.

penis; *American*

> Why don't you come on over here and pet my **one-eyed snake**?

> I used to call it stroking the salami, yeah, you know, pounding the old pud. I never did it with baked goods, but you know your Uncle Mort, he pets the **one-eyed snake** five to six times a day.
> —*American Pie*

one-night stand, n.

the act of sleeping with someone for a night with no intentions of anything beyond that one night; *American*

> After our **one-night stand**, I asked her if she wanted some coffee, and she said, "No! Stop smothering me!" I was glad this would be the only time that I ever slept with her.

> Michael: I'm not a **one-night stand** kinda guy, I don't like lying to women.
> Gob: These are lawyers. That's Latin for liar.
> —*Arrested Development*

open for lunch, adj.

unzipped fly; *American*

> Whoa there buddy, this may be a twenty-four-hour diner but you're the one **open for lunch**.

....

oral sex, n.

the act of performing oral intercourse on another person's genitals; *American*

> My girlfriend performs **oral sex** on me only after she has watched her TV shows; she's a romantic.

Synonyms of Oral Sex:

6-to-9
bagpipe
bite the big one
bj
blow the horn
blow the pipe
cock sucking
coitus per os
dick licking
dick taster
dinner at 6:09
eating corn
exploring the triangle forest
face artist
fast food sex
flute player
French lessons
giving head
going down
going downtown
going downstairs
gum job
head
head hunter
irrumation
jaw festivities
lipstick on the dipstick

lollipop lick
lost in face
mouth blast
mouth deep
mouth fuck
mouth love
mouth parade
mouth worker
oral coitus
oral exam
orogenitalism
penilingus
penosugia
phallalingus
pussy diving
Route 69
sixty-niner
sucking cock
sucking it
sucking the rail
suck off
swallow
sword swallower
talking into the microphone
vacuum cleaner
virilingus

orchard, n.

two or more sisters with nice asses; *American*

> When those **sisters with the orchards** walk down the street, heads turn.

oreo, n.

African American who has adopted white values and culture or "acts" white; *American*

> I used to like hanging out with Dwayne, but since he started going to that private Catholic school he's become a total **oreo**.

> **DERIVATION:** Oreo comes from the Oreo brand of chocolate cookie with a cream-filling—black on the outside and white on the inside.

orgasm, n.

climax; *American*

> The **orgasm** is not the end all and be all of sex, it just feels that way.

> You know what the French call an **orgasm**? *La petite morte.* "The Little Death." Come on, Tiffany. Let's die a little.
> —*Bride of Chucky*

orgasmic, adj.

delicious; wonderful; *American*

> Yum—these garlic mashed potatoes are positively **orgasmic**.

orgylicious, adj.

two or more people attractive enough for an orgy; *American*

> Despite the anorexia, those Olsen twins are **orgylicious**.

out (of the closet), adj.
openly homosexual; *American*

> It's none of my business really, but if my drama teacher came **out of the closet** I would not be terribly surprised.

to out, v.
to expose someone's homosexuality; *American*

> *Out* magazine has **outed** celebrities like Jodie Foster and Anderson Cooper—no surprise there.

out of one's tree, adj.
crazy; *British*

> He did too many mushrooms, mate, and was **out of his tree**.

> He did too many mushrooms, dude, and was **crazy**.

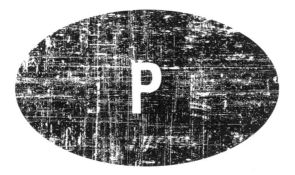

pack a bowl, v.

to fill a toilet bowl with a large amount of feces; *American*

> Jasmine had an extra bowl of chili last night for dinner and got up around midnight to **pack a bowl**.

pack a bowl, v.

to place weed into a bong or pipe in order to smoke cannabis; *American*

> If you're going to **pack a bowl** at your friend's house, you better ask him before you do it.

package, n.

penis; *American*

> My sister had a great time on her **package** tour to Morocco—good thing she left her boyfriend at home.

packie, v.
liquor store (used primarily in New England); *American*

> Jason ran out of whiskey on a Sunday night and had a panic attack because when he drove to the **packie**, it was closed.

packing, v.
to carry a concealed gun; *American*

> I wouldn't be out on the streets here after midnight if I were you. Everybody these days is **packing**.

packing a gun and a holster, v.
to be a hermaphrodite; *American*

> When she told me that she'd been born **packing a gun and a holster**, I really hoped she rid herself of the penis and kept the vagina.

> When she was born, she was **packing both a gun and a holster**.
> —*Freaks and Geeks*

to paddle the pink canoe, v.
female masturbation; *American*

> I was somewhat confused, then aroused, when I caught my girlfriend **paddling the pink canoe** to a video of her masturbating.

Paddy, n.
derogatory word for Irishman; *British*

> Whoa, **Paddy**, why don't you watch where you spill that beer!

> Whoa, **Irish asshole**, why don't you watch where you spill that beer!

> **DERIVATION:** Paddy is short for Patrick, one of the most common men's names in Ireland.

painal, adj.
painful anal sex; *American*

> Looking back to my first gay experience, one word describes it all—**painal**.

pansexual, n.
a person who is sexually attracted to others regardless of their sex or gender; *American*

> Because Ginger is a **pansexual**, I never know what pronoun to use when I refer to her partner.

panty hamster, n.
vagina; *American*

> I prefer a good time with a gerbil, but animal lover that I am, I'd make friends with a **panty hamster** if I were horny enough.

paps, n.
paparazzi; *American*

> Have you heard? Angelina Jolie is supposedly pregnant again and the **paps** are camped outside her compound in the south of France.

parentnoia, n.
paranoia a parent feels with regards to their children; *American*

> Cindy's mom had such a bad case of **parentnoia** that she read Cindy's diary to find out whether her daughter was still a virgin or not.

pash and dash, n.

one-night stand; *Australian*

> I thought when Samara and I hooked up we'd spend the rest of our lives together, but it was just a **pash and dash**.

> I thought when Samara and I hooked up we'd spend the rest of our lives together, but it was just a **one-night stand**.

> **DERIVATION:** Pash is short for passion.

pash rash, n.

rash from kissing an unshaved man; *Australian*

> My lazy husband never bothers to shave even though kissing him gives me a terrible **pash rash.**

> My lazy husband never bothers to shave even though kissing him gives me a terrible **rash**.

pecker, n.

penis; *American*

> Hannah was so impressed with her science class partner's **pecker**, she told all her friends about it.

> Shut up and keep your hands to yourself, or I'll cut your little **pecker** off.
> —*Sin City*

pedophilia, n.

mental disorder involving attraction to children; *American*

> Many Catholics claimed the abuse scandals that rocked the church were bogus—after all, the victims were post-pubescent, so clearly it wasn't a case of **pedophilia**.

penicorn, n.

mythical giant penis; *American*

> Every night before I go to bed I pray that someday my magical **penicorn** will come, and I'll come too.

....

penis, n.

male reproductive organ; *American*

> Mary was shocked at the size of John's **penis**; she didn't realize they came that small.

Synonyms of Penis:

5.9	dokey
34-25	dome piece
baloney pony	dong
beef hammer	donkey rope
bell on a pole	dork
boa	doty
bossman	dragon
bratwurst	dugan
bud	egg roll
cack	family jewels
Captain Winkie	fang
chang a lang	flesh arrow
chank	foo-foo
chep	fuck rod
choad	fuck stick
chopper	gadoon
chub	German sausage
chut	god warrior
coque	goot
the D	hang dang
dickie	hard hat
dicky mo	Harry Wang
Diesl	heat-seeking love missile
ding-a-ling	heli
dingis	hocky cocky
doder	hoftie
dog head	hog
doinker	horn »»»

Synonyms of Penis (continued)

hose
injector
inserter
Italian sausage
jimber
Jimmy
jizz rod
journey stick
joystick
juice cord
kontol
Krull the Warrior King
kur
Larry
leaky hose
lingham
little Elvis
the little head
little soldier
lizard
Logan
long john
longfellow
love shaft
love stick
male member
male organ
man cheddar
man crank
man horn
man meat
meat stick
meat train
member
microphone
middle stump
Mr. Happy
monkey
murton
mushroom head
mutton
my Army stick

my little pony
my other half
my other head
my twig (and berries)
NOFL
old boy
old fellow
old man
one-eyed monster
one-eyed trouser snake
one-eyed yogurt chucker
p-nas
packer
peen
peeper
pene
peter
phallus member
piece
pik
pingy-lingy
pink link
pinto
pipesicle
Pippen the Great
Pippen the Small
piss weasel
piston
pole
power drill
private eye
purple people pleaser
purple-headed soldier man
purple-headed warrior
purple-helmeted warrior of love
pussy factory
rod of pleasure
rubbing machine
salamander
schlittle
schlort
schmeckel ›››

Synonyms of Penis (continued)

schmuck	tonk
schu-bunny	tool
sconge	tube steak
scrotum	wand of light
short arm	wang
skin chimney	wankie
snake	weenie
soup bone	wee-wee
spam popsicle	weiner
sperm pump	whang
spike	who who dilly
Staff Captain	wii
steamin' semen roadway	willy
stick	Wilson
summer sausage	wing dang doodle
Tallyrand	wingwong
tassle	winky
thing	ying-yang
third leg	yogurt gun
thumper	you're welcome
tinky	

percy, n.
penis; *British*

> Adam's **percy** is a bit on the small side if you ask me.

> Adam's **penis** is a bit on the small side if you ask me.

perp, n.
fake crack made of wax and baking soda; *American*

> Instead of making dough Christmas ornaments to sell for the Red Cross, our girl scout troop made **perp** ornaments instead. We raised more than double this year!

personalities, n.
breasts; *British*

> Adrienne's **personalities** are her best asset.

> Adrienne's **boobs** are her best asset.

perv, n.
someone who is interested in deviant sexual behavior; *American*

> Your uncle is a **perv**—he totally checked me out at your granddad's funeral. Can I have his number?

to pet the poodle, v.
female masturbation; *American*

> Once again, Tim came too early and I was left to **pet the poodle** while he snored.

phat, adj.
cool; *American*

> Your new jeans are **phat**! Diesel or Abercrombie?

pickle park, n.
rest stop or area where men go to have unattached sex with each other; *American*

> Whatever you do, don't stop at rest stop nine on Highway One—it's a regular **pickle park.**

piece of piss, adj.
easy as pie; *British*

That final math exam was a **piece of piss**, especially because I wasn't hung over for the first time this semester.

That final math test was **easy as pie**, especially because I wasn't hung over for the first time this semester.

It must be a lot easier being gay. Sex must be a **piece of piss** if you're gay.
—*Coupling*

pig, n.
policeman; *American*

Why is it again that **pigs** love donuts?

You hear what he did there, Joe? He called us **pigs**, but in like a roundabout kinda way.
—*Dragnet*

pig out, v.
to overeat; *American*

Tracy always **pigs out** on chocolate and ice cream when she's PMSing.

pig-sticking, v.
to pursue overweight women with the intention of meaningless sexual intercourse, often as a bet or dare; *American*

Every first Friday of the month, my brother and his friends go **pig-sticking** just for fun—if I had my way I'd cut the bastards' dicks off.

piles, n.
hemorrhoids; *British*

> The worst thing about being up the duff is the **piles**.

> The worst thing about being knocked up is the **hemorrhoids**.

pillock, n.
fool; *British*

> Catherine, you **pillock**, don't forget to lock the door this time when you go out for your booty call.

> Catherine, you **fool**, don't forget to lock the door this time when you go out for your booty call.

pillow biter, n.
homosexual; *American*

> During our stay at the Holiday Inn during Pride Week, we had to change rooms because the **pillow biters** next door didn't seem to be biting into their pillows hard enough.

pill-popper, n.
drug addict; *American*

> I always thought Grandma was just the nervous type, but when she died I found a massive bottle of OxyContin in that **pill-popper's** purse.

pimp, n.

a man who manages prostitutes, taking a cut of their earnings; a guy who gets a lot of girls; *American*

> The **pimp** beat up two of his girls when they didn't give him half of the money they made.

> The way you're dressed, you're either a **pimp** or a limo driver.
> —*Be Cool*

to pimp (out), v.

to make over something in an over-the-top way; *American*

> Check out that **pimped-out** low rider with the fuzzy dice hanging from the rearview mirror.

> **DERIVATION:** Popularized by the MTV show *Pimp My Ride*.

pink posse, n.

group of gay male friends; *American*

> When the **pink posse** sashayed into the macho sports bar, all heads turned to witness a first.

pink sock, n.

rectal prolapse; *American*

> After years of hot guy on guy action, Bruno paid to have his genital warts frozen off, but kept his **pink sock** as a sentimental souvenir.

pink taco, n.
vagina; *American*

> Mercedes and I went for a picnic, but that slut didn't cook and insisted I eat her **pink taco.**

....

pink truffle, n.
vagina; *American*

> Mary likes a man who knows his way around a **pink truffle**.

....

pipe, v.
to copulate; *American*

> When I think about **piping** my Polish plumber, my pussy feels like it has sprung a leak.

....

piquerism, n.
sexual disorder involving mutilation; *American*

> Jack the Ripper suffered from a bad case of **piquerism**—after slitting his victim's throats, he mutilated their abdomens.

....

piss, v.
to urinate; *American*

> I didn't want to stop to take a leak, so I just **pissed** in a bottle while I was driving.

> **DERIVATION:** Piss comes from the vulgar Latin *pissiare,* meaning to urinate. The French call a public urinal a *pissoir*; the perjorative *pissant* is a combination of *pismire* and *ant.* A *pismire* is an ant, named for the foul smell of its urine.

piss off, v.

to anger; to get lost; *American*

> When you tell your wife she's fat, don't be surprised if you **piss** her **off** so much she tells you to **piss off**.

Can you **piss off** a Puerto Rican and live to tell about it?
—*Jennifer Lopez*

piss-ant, adj.

insignificant; *American*

> That **piss-ant** basketball player couldn't dribble his way out of a barn.

Well, it got so that every **piss-ant** prairie punk who thought he could shoot a gun would ride into town to try out the Waco Kid. I must have killed more men than Cecil B. DeMille.
—*Blazing Saddles*

pissed off, adj.

upset; *American*

> I know you're **pissed off** that I forgot to pick you up from school today.

pisser, n.

jerk; bummer; toilet; *American*

> What a **pisser** that **pisser** passed out in your **pisser**.

piss-poor, adj.

substandard; *American*

> This Kate Spade knock-off is a **piss-poor** substitute for the real handbag.

piss-up, n.

the act of drinking heavily at a bar or pub; *British*

> My roommate in college was English, and it was always awkward when he asked if I wanted to go for a **piss-up**—made me think he wanted to spend time peeing together.

> My roommate in college was English, and it was always awkward when he asked if I wanted to go **get piss drunk**—made me think he wanted to spend time peeing together.

pit job, n.

the act of masturbating oneself in a person's armpit; *American*

> If your girlfriend refuses a titty fuck, you might try asking for the less common **pit job**.

pitch a tent, v.

to get an erection; *American*

> Trevor **pitched a tent** in class and everyone noticed—including his bootylicious teacher.

pity fuck, v., n.

to have sexual intercourse out of pity; *American*

> Milo is a total loser and I have to dump him soon, but poor thing, I'd better give him one last **pity fuck**.

pity whore, n.

someone who constantly seeks the pity of others; *American*

> Don't listen to Marie's sob story about never having an orgasm; she's just a **pity whore**.

plank, n.
fool; *British*

> With her track record, only a **plank** would be in a relationship with her.

> With her track record, only a **fool** would be in a relationship with her.

plastered, adj.
drunk; *American*

> Let's buy a couple of wine coolers and get **plastered** tonight, okay?

play chopsticks, v.
mutual male masturbation; *American*

> The concert pianist was something of a snob and refused to **play chopsticks** with admiring fans.

play with oneself, v.
to masturbate; *American*

> Shoshanna was **playing with herself** when her boyfriend walked in and joined the game.

played out, adj.
unfashionable, no longer cool; *American*

> I can't believe you're going to wear a tight miniskirt . . . that look is so **played out**.

player, n.

a man who goes out or sleeps with many different women; *American*

Todd slept with three girls this week? What a **player**!

*You don't play a **player**.*
—Firefly

plonker, n.

dummy; dick; *British*

If he weren't such a **plonker**, Stu would be able to fully appreciate the fit birds with the nice booties at the pub.

If he weren't such a **dummy**, Stu would be able to fully appreciate the sexy girls with the nice booties at the bar.

plow, v.

to have sexual intercourse; *American*

I can't believe that sick fuck in South Carolina **plowed** a horse—weren't there any hot sheep around?

PnP, n.

drug use followed by gay sex; *American*

Every Saturday night without fail, it's **PnP** for the pink posse.

DERIVATION: PnP stands for "plug and party."

pocket nymph, n.

a sexy, petite girl to put in one's pocket, bring home, and turn into a sex slave; *American*

At the bar there was this little **pocket nymph** I just wanted to throw in my shirt pocket and declare war on at my place.

pocket pool, n.

when a man masturbates himself through the pocket of his pants in public; *American*

> At the rink last week, I saw some old perv sitting on a bench playing **pocket pool** while he watched the ice skaters.

poke, v.

to copulate; *American*

> How many friends on Facebook have you **poked** this week?

pokesack, n.

scrotum; *American*

> For a better blow job, open your mouth wide to suck the whole **pokesack.**

poofy, adj.

effeminate; *British*

> Get rid of that **poofy** moustache. This is the army, not the Blue Oyster Cult.

> Get rid of that **effeminate** moustache. This is the army, not the Blue Oyster Cult.

poon/poontang, n.

pussy; *American*

> Last night I got so much **poontang** at the local brothel. That's why I'm in jail today.
>
> **DERIVATION:** This is similar to one of the many French words for prostitute, *putain*. Both these terms come from the old French *pute*, meaning "rotten."

....

poontang plantation, n.

brothel; *American*

> For every sweet ass hooker walking the streets of Bangkok, there are a hundred waiting in local **poontang plantations**.

pop a nut, v.

to ejaculate; *American*

> Despite his best intentions, Casey **popped his nut** inside his girlfriend a little too soon for her taste.

pop someone's cherry, v.

to break the hymen on a virgin's vagina; *American*

> Ricky **popped his girlfriend's cherry** and it stained the sheets. She made him change them.

....

poppers, n.

inhalable drugs often used to relax the sphincter; *American*

> For first time anal fun, I'd recommend some **poppers** and an enema beforehand.

porker, n.
overweight person; *American*

> My ex had a big dick but he was such a **porker** you had to dig between his rolls to find it.

pornstache, n.
mustache often worn by actors in pornographic films; *American*

> Shave that **pornstache** or I may never be able to look you in the eye or fuck you again.

posse, n.
group of friends, clique, gang; *American*

> T-bone and his **posse** spent the night drinking forties and smoking dope.

pound, v.
to copulate; *American*

> If my boyfriend **pounds** me hard enough, I swear I can taste his cum in my mouth.

pound the duck, v.
to have sexual intercourse; *American*

> Cliff is a vegetarian but still **pounds the duck** once a week for good health.

povo, adj.
broke; *Australian*

> My motherfucking paycheck bounced and now I'm totally **povo**.

> My motherfucking paycheck bounced and now I'm totally **broke**.

prairie dog, v.
to stand up in one's cubicle and peer out to view any excitement; *American*

> When the CEO yelled at me, all of the other workers **prairie dogged** me. It was so embarrassing.

prannet, n.
idiot, tool; *British*

> He's such a **prannet** that he probably needs a road map to find his wife's vagina.

> He's such an **idiot** that he probably needs a road map to find his wife's vagina.

prat, n.
jerk; *British*

> If you don't stop acting like a **prat**, I will never role play as a sexy French maid with a lisp again!

> If you don't stop acting like a **jerk**, I will never role play as a sexy French maid with a lisp again!

You are a pea-brained, **prat-faced**, pompous, pillock-headed cretin. If you took an intensive course of intelligence injections and studied till you drop, then one day you might make it to moron third class failed.
—*Chef!*

preggers, adj.
pregnant; *American*

> Janine wanted to get **preggers** with Michael's baby desperately, but he refused to come in anything but her ass.

premature ejaculation, n.
when a man ejaculates before inserting his penis into his partner's vagina; *American*

> Brian bought a Sybian for his wife to make up for his constant **premature ejaculation**.

premature evacuation, n.
being caught trying to sneak away after a one night stand; *American*

> When he didn't realize how much he had drank and knocked into a wall, Todd woke up the chick he had slept with and suffered a **premature evacuation**.

prick, n.
penis; jerk; *American*

> Dating Rule #1: Once a **prick**, always a dick.

> Cobb is a **prick**. But he sure can hit. God Almighty, that man can hit.
> —*Babe Ruth*

Prick peddler, n.
hustler; *American*

> After a stint in the joint, my dad took up the only work he could find—as a **prick peddler**.

prick purse, n.
vagina; *American*

> Spread your lips and open your **prick purse** wide or you won't get that hundred I promised you.

pricknic, n.
gay orgy preferably outdoors in the summer; *American*

> Stay out of the park after sunset, kids, there's many a **pricknic** come summertime.

prick-tease, n.
person who leads a man on; *American*

> Beth delighted in bending over in front of her colleagues whenever she had the chance, but HR was not impressed with the office **prick-tease**.

prig, n.
a smug, annoying person, typically male; *American*

> Don't be such a self-righteous **prig**, Rush, and try to at least consider another point of view.

privates, n.
genitals; *American*

> Listen son, if anyone tries to touch your **privates**, you scream for help, okay?

procrasterbating, v.

to masturbate as a means of procrastination; *American*

> I really should stop **procrasterbating** when I'm trying to write a paper for school because my papers end up with cum stains.

prostitot, n.

an underage girl who dresses like a whore; *American*

> Mikey's little sister came in from school with a belly shirt and the shortest skirt ever, looking like a total **prostitot**.

pub crawl, n.

visiting numerous bars in one evening; *American*

> In Rome, Kati and I went on a fantastic **pub crawl**—it cost only ten euros each and we were totally wasted by the end of the night.

pubes, n.

pubic hair; *American*

> I went to a cheap whorehouse while I was in Reno, and I'm not sure if there were more **pubes** in the shower drain or the hooker's teeth.

pudd, n.

penis; *American*

> Quit playing with your **pudd** in public! There's a family over there!

> **DERIVATION:** Pudd comes from the Yiddish word for penis.

pudding pop, n.
penis covered in a sticky layer of feces after anal sex; *American*

> Ira finally realized his dream of anal sex, but wasn't sure the pleasure of a tight asshole outweighed the disgusting clean up of his **pudding pop** afterward.

puffing, v.
blowing air into a woman's vagina; *American*

> **Puffing** can be fun, but watch out for some nasty queefs later on.

pug noshing, v.
cunnilingus; *British*

> I shouldn't have risked **pug noshing** after a Sunday morning fry-up; I'm not sure if it was the bacon or her twat that made me vomit.

> I shouldn't have risked **going down** on her after a Sunday morning breakfast; I'm not sure if it was the bacon or her twat that made me vomit.

puke, v.
to vomit; *American*

> When he shoved his pudding pop into my mouth, I wanted to **puke**.

Don't **puke** on the C-4.
—*Chuck*

pull, v.

to make out; to hit on; *British*

> You should try to **pull** Claire; she's well up for a bit of you.
>
> You should try to **make out** with Claire; she's totally into you.

pull a bumblebee, v.

to use a vibrator; *American*

> Sandra is **pulling a bumblebee** in the ladies room.
>
> **DERIVATION:** The buzzing sound some noisy vibrators make resembles that of a bumblebee.

pull a Kanye, v.

to voice an arrogant opinion only later to realize you acted like a jerk; *American*

> Don't **pull a Kanye**! Just keep your opinions to yourself.
>
> **DERIVATION:** This phrase is taken from when Kanye West interrupted Taylor Swift's acceptance speech at the 2009 MTV Video Music Awards to state that Beyoncé's video should have won.

> I realize that my place and position in history is that I will go down as the voice of this generation, of this decade.
> —*Kanye West*

pull a train, v.

to have sexual intercourse in a line, with one person "pulling" the others; *American*

> **Pulling a train** can be a shitload of fun, but it's also hard on the knees.

pull ass, v.
to have sexual intercourse; *American*

I **pulled ass** at my brother's wedding without even having to buy a girl a drink.

pull in one's horns, v.
to stop pestering someone with a hard-on; *American*

Pull in your horns! If I catch you rubbing your nasty hard-on on my leg again I'll scream.

pullers, n.
crack addicts who pull at their body parts obsessively; *American*

Pushers and **pullers**, that's all the crack scene has to offer—besides crack whores, of course.

pumpers, n.
steroids; *American*

Arnie's muscles may be ginormous, but all those **pumpers** have left his putz looking like an overboiled sausage.

punch drunk love, n.
love that makes one feel dazed, confused, or bewildered; *American*

Punch drunk love must've been the reason for my dating Siobhan. Nothing else could explain why I let that bitch walk all over me.

Paul Thomas Andersen's film of the same name brought comedy star Adam Sandler kudos for his stellar portrayal of a man punch drunk in love.

punch up the bracket, v.

punch in the face; *British*

Touch my wife again and you'll get a **punch up the bracket**, arsehole!

Touch my wife again and you'll get a **punch in the face**, asshole!

pusher, n.

drug dealer; *American*

When I grow up, I wanna be a **pusher** or a whore—I can't make up my mind.

pussfuck, n.

annoying, pimply teenager; *American*

Tell that **pussfuck** boyfriend of yours to get his car out of my parking spot or I'll slash his tires.

pussy, n.

vagina; wimp; *American*

Shut up, Dick, and lick my **pussy** now!

The Owl looked up to the Stars above
And sang to a small guitar,
"Oh lovely **Pussy**! O **Pussy**, my love,
What a beautiful **Pussy** you are."
—*Edward Lear*

pussy-whipped, adj.

a man or woman who does everything their partner wants; *American*

His wife makes him cook every night? Dude, Toby is **pussy-whipped**.

No, wait a minute. You have to "get" the **pussy** before you can be **whipped** by it.
—*Waiting*

put out, v.

to have sexual intercourse with; *American*

Tune in, turn on, **put out**—that's what those free-love hippies should've been saying.

put the cat in the box, v.

to copulate; *American*

Sweetie, my pussy's all wet—can you **put the cat in the box** as soon as possible?

putz, n.

dick; fool; *American*

Put your **putz** back in your pants before the teacher catches you, okay?

DERIVATION: This term is one of several Yiddish terms for penis that has found a place in American vernacular.

putz around, v.

to act foolishly or waste time; *American*

> Stop **putzing around** and take off your panties; I've only got a twenty-minute lunch break.

....

pweenis, n.

small penis; *American*

> Aw, look at that cute little **pweenis**. No, of course you're not too small for me, sweetie!

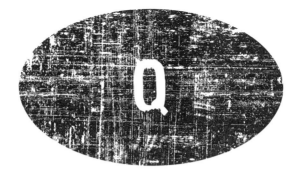

quack, n.
bad, poorly trained doctor; *American*

> Oscar needs a hip replacement but won't let that **quack** near him.

queef, n.
vaginal fart; *American*

> I was about to go down on Megan until she let out this tiny **queef** in my face; it sounded like a little air being released from a balloon.

> I love the smell of **queef** in the morning.
> —*Dodgeball: A True Underdog Story*

queen, n.
effeminate homosexual man; *American*

> The band Queen was led by one of the greatest **queens** of all time, Freddie Mercury.

queen of hearts, n.
homosexual heartbreaker; *American*

> Marvin knew better than to fall for Grant's charms—the best he'd get from that **queen of hearts** was a one-night stand.

queer, n.
homosexual; *American*

> No wonder Lenny pushed Susanne away when she tried to French him—he's a **queer**!

> If homosexuality is a disease, let's all call in **queer** to work: "Hello. Can't work today, still **queer**."
> —*Robin Tyler*

queer as a three dollar bill, adj.
overtly homosexual; *American*

> You didn't realize Larry is gay? C'mon, he's **queer as a three dollar bill**.

quickie, n.
quick round of sex; *American*

> Jeremy caught his mom and dad having a **quickie** in the kitchen. He's had nightmares ever since.

> With you, never a **quickie**. Always a longie.
> —*Love at First Bite*

Quigley down under, n.
sexual intercourse with an Australian; *American*

> Nicole Kidman? Pass. Naomi Watts? Oh yeah, I'd be in for a bit of **Quigley down under** with her all right.

R-2, n.
"rufies"; rohypnol; the so-called "date-rape" drug; *American*

> Those freaks at the *Star Wars* convention may seem harmless, but last year an R2D2 impersonator tried to put an **R-2** into my drink, so I kicked that trash bucket over.

rack, n.
breasts; *American*

> That's some **rack** Marilyn Monroe had, I'll tell you.

Top Ten Hollywood Racks

1. Marilyn Monroe
2. Scarlett Johansson
3. Mae West
4. Salma Hayek
5. Sophia Loren
6. Halle Berry
7. Jane Russell
8. Tyra Banks
9. Dolly Parton
10. Pamela Anderson

rag on (someone), v.
to criticize someone; *American*

> Stop **ragging on** me, Mom! I said I'd clean my room and I will!

rainbow kiss, n.

the act of going down on a woman when she is having her period; *American*

> I bet vampires have a fetish for giving **rainbow kisses**.

ram, v.

to copulate; *American*

> I'd love to suck off that quarterback and let him **ram** me good and hard.

rancid, adj.

ugly; *American*

> No offense, but your new girlfriend is **rancid**. How do you fuck her without putting a paper bag over her head?

randy, adj.

horny; *British*

> I'm so **randy**, I'd fuck a horse . . . wait, that's not how the saying goes.

> I'm so **horny**, I'd fuck a horse . . . wait, that's not how the saying goes.

> Let me ask you a question. And be honest. Do I make you horny, baby? Do I? Do I make you **randy**?
> —*Austin Powers: The Spy Who Shagged Me*

raw jaws, n.

when someone's mouth is tired from copious amounts of oral sex; *American*

> When I came back from holiday in Greece, I had such a bad case of the **raw jaws** that I was on a liquid diet for a whole month.

razz, n.
puke; *British*

> Yuck! I've still got **razz** on my pants from that guy who didn't know his alcohol limits last night.

> Yuck! I've still got **puke** on my pants from that guy who didn't know his alcohol limits last night.

read Braille, v.
to finger a woman's vagina; *American*

> Blind men like Andrea Bocelli are so hot—and they know how to **read Braille** correctly.

relaced, adj.
said of a gay man who has tried women for a period of time only to return to his homosexual ways; *American*

> Thank God Pat is **relaced**. Now I suggest you give him the best blow job of his life, lest he again fall off the wagon.

restroom, n.
break room; *British*

> Take a whiz in the **restroom** and you'll be sacked immediately.

> Take a whiz in the **break room** and you'll be fired immediately.

reverse missionary, n.

sexual position with one partner face down and the other on top in the missionary position; *American*

> To spice things up sweetie, we could maybe start with the **reverse missionary** or even just a blow job if you're game?

Richard, n.

poop, turd; *British*

> Move aside, I've got a **Richard** brewing that's likely to sound like an atomic bomb when it drops.

> Move aside, I've got a **turd** brewing that's likely to sound like an atomic bomb when it drops.

> Listen, I just laid a **Richard** Longfellow in there. It took four flushes to take the motherfucker to the next dimension.
> —*The Road To Dogtown*

ricockulous, adj.

ridiculous; American

> Break up with her just because she gives a lousy blowjob? Don't be silly, that's **ricockulous**.

> **DERIVATION:** This term was popularized by Adam Carolla on his Loveline radio show with Dr. Drew in the '90s.

to ride, v.

to have sex; *American*

> Watch me **ride** the entire football team by the end of the season!

> Like you could **ride** me until my knees buckled. Squeeze me 'til I pop like warm champagne. That's not the kind of thing a man forgets.
> —*Buffy the Vampire Slayer*

ride sidesaddle, v.

when a homosexual man has intercourse with a woman; *American*

> Putting aside his true desire for gay sex, the hairdresser made a compromise and **rode sidesaddle** instead.

to ride the pink pony, v.

to copulate; *American*

> Adam and Steve **ride the pink pony** every day after happy hour.

ridin' dirty, n.

driving with illegal goods or drugs in one's car; *American*

> Don't let the pigs pull you over when you're **ridin' dirty** or you'll do jail time.

Krayzie Ridin'

If you're really into ridin' dirty, check out the classic Grammy-winning Chamillionaire song "Ridin'," which features rapper Krayzie Jones.

rimmadonna, n.

someone who enjoys and performs frequent rim jobs; *American*

> My dislike for the taste of shit is the only thing holding me back from **rimmadonna** status.

road head, n.

blow job while driving; *American*

> Give you **road head**—have you lost your mind? You can barely concentrate during rush hour as it is.

to rock and roll, v.

to have sexual intercourse; *American*

> When I've got the blues, only **rock and roll** will do.

....

rock star, n.

crack whore; *American*

> **Rock stars** and cock stars go together like peanut butter and jelly.

....

rod, n.

penis; *American*

> The only interesting part of our fishing trip was my buddy's lengthy **rod**. Thankfully I didn't catch anything.

Dennis Rodman was perhaps the most appropriately named basketball star of all time. After dating Madonna and Carmen Electra, he admitted to sleeping with men as well.

to rodger, v.

to have anal sex; *British*

> Oscar **rodgered** Bernadette and she couldn't walk the next day.

> Oscar **ass-fucked** Bernadette and she couldn't walk the next day.

Roman shower, n.

the act of vomiting on someone to stimulate sexual arousal; *American*

> Careful during your spring break trip to Italy—if your hotel room doesn't have a bathtub, don't let the owner talk you into a **Roman shower**.

to root, v.
to have sex; *Australian*

> Avoid the toilets in the park after sundown. There are always a few blokes **rooting** in there.

> Avoid the toilets in the park after sundown. There are always a few dudes **having sex** in there.

ropey, adj.
ill or sick, often due to liquor; *British*

> After all that Guinness Alex drank, I'm not surprised he feels **ropey**.

> After all that Guinness Alex drank, I'm not surprised he feels **sick**.

rough, adj.
ugly; *British*

> That bird's as **rough** as nails, but she's rich so I see no reason why she couldn't at least be a sugar momma.

> That girl is **ugly** as shit, but she's rich so I see no reason why she couldn't at least be a sugar momma.

rub one out, v.
to jerk off; *American*

> He was watching a porno and **rubbing one out** when the power went out.

rubber fuckie, n.

vibrating rubber duckie; *American*

> My sister only uses her **rubbie fuckie** when she is tired of her normal dildo.

rumpy-pumpy, n.

sex; *British*

> I would enjoy a nice spot of **rumpy-pumpy** with her.

> I would like to have **sex** with her.

Rx: Rumpy-Pumpy

A forty-two-year-old Dublin doctor was accused of malpractice after advising one of his insomniac patients to indulge in a little rumpy-pumpy to help her sleep. "Find a willy and have some sex," Dr. Ross Shane Ardill apparently told the woman, who later filed a complaint. The good doctor was cleared of all charges.

"Kinky **rumpy-pumpy**" is what my sergeant would call it.
—*Inspector Morse*

rusty trombone, n.

the act of licking a man's anus while simultaneously reaching around and jerking him off; *American*

> Violet played the cello beautifully but refused to play the **rusty trombone**.

So I was about to **rusty trombone** the john when I found out he had not bathed in a few days. Forget that!
—*Splendor In The Ass*

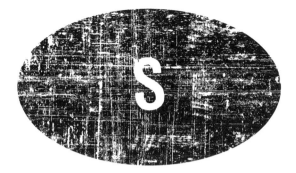

S&M, n.
sadism and masochism; *American*

> Jack and Jill may look like the All-American couple, but behind the closed doors of their classic Cape Cod home, they're totally into **S&M**.

Sade & Masoch

S&M takes its name from two princes of penis envy, the Marquis de Sade and Leopold von Sacher-Masoch. The Marquis de Sade was a sexually obsessed eighteenth-century writer who glorified the pleasure of inflicting pain on one's sexual partner in his life as well as in such works as *Justine*, *Juliette*, and *The 120 Days of Sodom*. Arrested more than once for his writing and his actions, Sade spent much of his life in the asylum and prison. The term Sadism comes from the French *sadisme,* inspired by the Marquis de Sade. The renowned Austrian "Father of Psychoanalysis" Sigmund Freud popularized the term in 1905 in his *Three Essays on the Theory of Sexuality*.

Von Sacher-Masoch, on the other hand, was a nineteenth-century Austrian journalist who played out his fantasies of sexual submission at home and on the page. His most famous "novel," *Venus in Furs*, tells the story of a man who persuades his wife to treat him as her slave with increasing degradation. (And yes, that eponymous song by The Velvet Undergound was inspired by this book.) The noted Austrian psychiatrist Richard Freiherr von Krafft-Ebing coined the term masochism after von Sacher-Masoch in his acclaimed treatise *Psychopathia Sexualis* in 1886.

to saddle up, v.

to perform anal sex; *American*

> Bend over baby, your cowboy is ready to **saddle up** and ride you all
> night long.

salami, n.

penis; *American*

> I blushed when the butcher asked me how big a **salami** I was in the
> mood for.

sascrotch, n.

a hairy, unkempt vagina that bears a striking
resemblance to Sasquatch; *American*

> Whoa! I've seen a lot of hairy snatches in 70s porn, but your
> **sascrotch** takes the cake.

sauce shelf, n.

woman's cleavage; *American*

> After just two minutes of sex, Dirk couldn't resist the urge to pull out and jizz
> on his date's **sauce shelf**.

sausage sandwich, n.

rubbing of a penis between two breasts; *American*

> Hello, I'd like a quarter-pounder with cheese and a **sausage sandwich** for
> dessert, if you know what I mean, miss.

scat, n.

sexual activity involving feces; *American*

> Thanks for your offer to shit on my face, but I'll have to pass—I'm not really into **scat**.

....

schlong, n.

penis; *American*

> Jake has a foot-long **schlong**; I can hardly get it all into my mouth.

> That's no bong. It's for my **schlong**.
> —*Van Wilder*

....

schmuck, n.

jerk; *Yiddish*

> Only a real **schmuck** would schtup your sister at your bar-mitzvah.
>
> **DERIVATION:** The word *schmuck* comes from the Yiddish meaning "penis".

> Yes, honey. The **schmuck**, who deserves to die, worries about you. Sometimes worrying about you feels like a full-time job.
> —*Something's Gotta Give*

schtup, v.

to have sex; *American*

> Check out Lili von **Schtup** in that classic Mel Brooks western, *Blazing Saddles*.
>
> **DERIVATION:** The word *schtup* comes from the Yiddish meaning "to press".

schwing, interj.

an expression meaning, roughly, "wow!" (usually used in a sexual context); *American*

> When the nubile young Nicole walks into a room, every guy thinks, "**Schwing**!"—but only Davie is lame enough to say it out loud.

> **DERIVATION:** Popularized in the *Wayne's World* films featuring *SNL* alums Mike Myers and Dana Carvey.

scissor fight, n.

lesbian sex act where two women intertwine their legs while pressing together their vaginas; *American*

> You should've seen the view from my bedroom window last night . . . my hot lesbian neighbors in a **scissor fight**.

sconner, n.

person with shaved pubic hair; *British*

> After that semester abroad in Germany, I feel like I've got a hairball the size of a rat in my throat. I can't wait to get back home and date only **sconners**.

> After that semester abroad in Germany, I feel like I've got a hairball the size of a rat in my throat. I can't wait to get back home and date only **girls who are shaved**.

score, v.

to have sex; *American*

> David Beckham would be the ultimate **score**, even for someone who hates soccer.

screenager, n.
teenager who spends too much time in front of a computer screen; *American*

> In my day, we didn't have computers or cell phones. Nowadays, these **screenagers** care more about checking their e-mail than getting laid.

screw, v.
to have sex; *American*

> Paul's **screwing** his blonde secretary? How bourgeois!

My reaction to porno films is as follows: After the first ten minutes, I want to go home and screw. After the first twenty minutes, I never want to **screw** again as long as I live.
—*Erica Jong*

screw up, v.
to mess up; *American*

> When Lonnie **screws up**, he **screws up** in a big way. That's why he's currently incarcerated.

Have fun, be crazy, be weird. Go out and **screw up**! You're going to anyway, so you might as well enjoy the process.
—*Anthony Robbins*

scromp, v.
to have sexual intercourse; *American*

> Try the backdoor one more time and there'll be no more **scromping** for you.

scumbag, n.

jerk; condom; *American*

> That **scumbag** Bobby always leaves his used **scumbags** lying around our dorm room.

> If the First Amendment will protect a **scumbag** like me, it will protect all of you.
> —*Larry Flynt*

seafood, n.

gay slang for a Navy or Marine corp officer; *American*

> Why don't we head down to the port tonight? There's a Navy ship just in and I'm in the mood for **seafood**.

see a man about a dog, v.

to go take a piss; *British*

> If you'll excuse me, ladies, I've got to **see a man about a dog**.

> If you'll excuse me, ladies, I've got **to use the restroom**.

semi, n.

semi-erect penis; *American*

> Roxana was ready to cream her panties but despite a rockin' blow job, Anthony could only manage a **semi**.

senioritis, n.

the lack of desire to attend school suffered by high school seniors the spring before graduation; *American*

> The principal just declared war on **senioritis**—any senior caught off school grounds during class hours will be suspended.

septic, n.
an American; *British*

> A British guy called all of us a bunch of stupid **septics** at the bar, so we laughed at him and I asked him, "What next? Are you going to call us a bunch of Yankees?"

> A British guy called all of us a bunch of stupid **Americans** at the bar, so we laughed at him and I asked him, "What next? Are you going to call us a bunch of Yankees?"

sex, n.
intercourse; gender; *American*

> **Sex** is a favorite extracurricular activity for all **sexes**.

> Is **sex** dirty? Only if it's done right.
> —*Woody Allen*

sex up, v.
to glamorize; *American*

> Sharlene always **sexes up** her life as a single woman whenever she talks to her married sister in Queens.

sexcellent, adj.
excellent with regards to sex; *American*

> How was my night with the biddy from across the hall? **Sexcellent!**

sexpert, n.
expert in the field of sex; *American*

> Dr. Ruth must be over a hundred years old, but she's still the **sexpert** with the best advice around.

sextasy, n.

the act of taking both ecstasy and Viagra simultaneously; *American*

> For middle-aged men who still go to raves, they might have **sextasy**, but that doesn't take away from their midlife crisis.

sexting, v.

sending nude photos via text; *American*

> Lorraine accidentally **sexted** four-color photos of her glorious double-Ds to her boss—instead of her boyfriend. She got a promotion.

shaft, n.

penis; *American*

> At nine inches, Rodney's **shaft** was just big enough to touch his lover's cervix with every deep thrust.

shafted, adj.

screwed over; *American*

> You were **shafted** on that promotion, man. You've worked overtime all year and never complained even once.

shag, v.

to have sex; *British*

There's nothing like **shagging** on a Sunday morning to start the Sabbath off right.

There's nothing like **fucking** on a Sunday morning to start the Sabbath off right.

Felicity Shagwell, CIA. **Shagwell** by name, **shag-very-well** by reputation.
—*Austin Powers: The Spy Who Shagged Me*

To Shag an Englishman

While the French may be known for their romantic ways and the Italians for their hot blood, the British may be the world's most underrated mates. Though they aren't known as particularly warm hearted or passionate lovers, recent surveys show they can indeed be counted on for a good *shag*. According to a *Men's Health* survey of over 40,000 men worldwide, British men spend more time on foreplay than any others, including the French and Italians. And, around one-third of them say they bring their partner to orgasm every time they do the deed. On the other hand, the British devote only eighteen minutes to sex itself, embarrassingly less than the Mexicans and Dutch. Which explains why the terms "Mexican jumping bean" and "Dutch treat" are still in use. . . .

shagbag, n.

promiscuous female or gay man; prostitute; *British*

It's not fair—when we go out on the pull, you always get the fit birds and I get stuck with the mangy **shagbags**.

It's not fair—when we go out on the make, you always get the hotties and I get stuck with the **ugly sluts**.

shaggable, adj.

worth having sex with; *British*

My mate's mum is a right MILF—more than just **shaggable**, really.

My mate's mum is a right MILF—more than just **worth having sex with**, really.

shake the snake, v.

to drain the lizard; to pee; *British*

> This lager's going straight through me. I've got to go **shake the snake** again.

> This beer's going straight through me. I've got to go **drain the lizard** again.

....

shambles, n.

a mess; *British*

> Pete's marriage wouldn't be in **shambles** if he got over his fetish for S&M brothels.

> Pete's marriage wouldn't be a **mess** if he got over his fetish for S&M brothels.

....

shank, v., n.

v. to stab; n. a makeshift knife;
American

> My friend spent a year in prison and almost got **shanked** by this guy who carved a knife from his toothbrush.

> Does not a warm handshake feel better than a cold . . . **shank**?
> —*Prison Break*

shark fin, n.

visible labia in a swimsuit; *American*

> Going to the beach with my mom is so embarrassing—she wears an old swimsuit from the eighties that gives her a **shark fin** you can spot from a mile away.

sharking, v.

the practice of pulling down an unsuspecting woman's pants, skirt, or panties in public; *American*

Hiroko came home in tears after a nasty **sharking** incident on the subway. If only she hadn't been on her period, she might not have been so embarrassed.

Sharking is extremely popular in Japan, where crowded streets, trains, and shops make for easy access to this degrading, yet hysterically funny, practice.

shed load, n.

shit load; *British*

There's a **shed load** of pinched bangers in East London.

There's a **shit load** of stolen cars in East London.

sheep shagger, n.

country dweller; *British*

Dwight had better learn to dress properly when he goes off to university in London, otherwise he'll be mocked as a **sheep shagger**.

Dwight had better learn to dress properly when he goes off to university in London, otherwise he'll be mocked as a **country dweller**.

she-hulk, n.

a giant, frighteningly veiny penis; *American*

I saw Fred in the locker room the other day out of the corner of my eye and his **she-hulk** hung past his knee; he could have killed me with it.

sheila, n.

chick, lady; *Australian*

> I've got three crates of beer and a bottle of sherry for the **sheilas**.

> I've got three crates of beer and a bottle of sherry for the **chicks**.

she-male, n.

male transsexual with breasts who has retained his penis; *American*

> I truly believe there is nothing sexier than a **she-male** with big fake titties and a long, hard dick.

shigga digga, interj.

to show enthusiastic agreement or appreciation; *American*

> Paul told me this awesome story and said, "Know what I mean, dude?" All I could muster was, "Fuckin' **shigga digga**, man."

shit, n.

feces; stuff; jerk; *American*

> I hated my college roommate Sam— he never cleaned up and left his **shit** all over the apartment.

> **DERIVATION:** The word shit comes from the Old English *scite*, meaning "dung."

> Boys, I may not know much, but I know chicken **shit** from chicken salad.
> —*Lyndon B. Johnson*

shit a brick, v.

to be extremely nervous; *American*

> Despite the fingerfucking beforehand, I still **shit a brick** the first time I let Dan go anal on me.

shit, dawg!, interj.

an expression meaning, roughly, "wow!"; *American*

> **Shit, dawg**! You are so fucked now that you got your ass fired.

shit happens, interj.

an expression that means, roughly, "that's life"; *American*

> The hipster existentialist says with all the wisdom of his sixteen years on earth, "**Shit happens**, man, because life sucks."

> You're young, you're drunk, you're in bed, you have knives; **shit happens**.
> —*Angelina Jolie*

shit list, n.

persona non grata; *American*

> Her lying, cheating ex-husband will be on Caroline's **shit list** for life.

shit on a stick, adj.

cool, great, fantastic; *British*

> You know what was **shit on a stick**? Bands usually stick the female of the group on any instrument but the guitar, but that fit bird was playing the guitar and rocking out.

> You know what was **great**? Bands usually stick the female of the group on any instrument but the guitar, but that biddy was playing the guitar and rocking out.

shit on someone, v.

to betray someone; *British*

Divorce is just one spouse **shitting on the other person** for the last time—only in court.

Divorce is just one spouse **betraying the other person** for the last time—only in court.

When a man pulls **shit on me** he is either very brave or very stoned. Which one are you?
—*52 Pick Up*

shite, n.

shit; *British*

I was drinking straight shots of Jameson last night. Today, I feel like **shite** and have had explosive whiskey diarrhea all day.

I was drinking straight shots of Jack Daniel's last night. Today, I feel like **shit** and have been taking whiskey shits all day.

It's **shite** being Scottish! We're the lowest of the low. The scum of the fucking Earth!
—*Trainspotting*

shit-faced, adj.

drunk; *American*

Pete came home totally **shit-faced** after a night of drinking with his old high school buddies.

shit-for-brains, n.

dummy; idiot; *American*

My boyfriend is a total **shit-for-brains**—he confused our anniversary with Christmas and wrote me a card saying "Merry Anniversary sweetie—Jesus loves you."

shithole, n.

messy or poor quality area; *American*

> Jan finally moved out of her parent's place, but all she could afford was a studio in the Bronx. Man, what a **shithole**.

....

shitkickers, n.

heavy boots; *American*

> Don't get me wrong, some Goth girls are hot, but why do they have to wear those ugly **shitkickers**?

shitstorm, n.

big mess; trouble; *American*

> If you don't dump out the ashtrays and put away your weed before Mom gets home there's going to be an absolute **shitstorm**.

> If you ever carried out your proposed threat you would experience such a **shitstorm** of consequences, my friend, your empty little head would be spinning faster than the wheels of your Schwinn bicycle back there.
> —*Burn After Reading*

shmonster, n.

general term for someone who isn't as good as you; combination of "shmuck" and "monster"; *American*

> The biddy with the swoops is way too good for that **shmonster**.

....

shoop, v.

to fuck; *American*

> **Shoop** to Barry White—and you'll **shoop** some more.

shoot the shit, v.
to make small talk; *American*

> Tom **shoots the shit** so much on the job that he ends up doing a lot of overtime to catch up—on his employer's dime.

shooting gallery, n.
place where injected drugs are used or sold; *American*

> Hell's Kitchen used to be a **shooting gallery**, but now lofts there sell for millions.

shop someone, v.
to snitch on someone; *British*

> That little rat **shopped me** for robbery. I'm going to rip his tongue out!

> That little rat **snitched on me** for robbery. I'm going to rip his tongue out!

short and curlies, n.
pubic hair; *American*

> Shave your bearded clam or I won't go down on you again. I'm tired of picking your **short and curlies** out of my teeth!

shorty, n.
attractive female; *American*

Hey **shorty**, how's about a taste of
your milkshake?

I roll up on that **shorty** be
like, "What's up yo?" she
be like, "You don't know
twenty different ways
to make me call you Big
Poppa" cuz I don't yo.
—*Can't Hardly Wait*

shout, n.
round of drinks; *British*

Mitch ordered another **shout** for the fit birds he was trying to seduce.
However, he was ordering them O'Douls and he soon left the bar that night,
sans ladies.

Mitch ordered another **round of drinks** for the biddies he was trying to
seduce. However, he was ordering them O'Douls and he left the bar that
night, sans ladies.

shove off, v.
to go away; to get lost; *British*

Tell that bloke who likes the New York Yankees to **shove off**—he probably
overcompensates for lack of a big bat by paying for his women with his over-
exaggerated salary.

Tell that dude who likes the New York Yankees to **get lost**—he probably
overcompensates for lack of a big bat by paying for his women with his over-
exaggerated salary.

show a hanky, v.
to be homosexual; *American*

I'm not saying Bob is gay, but he
shows a hanky.

A hanky can be a clever signal for gay
preferences. Worn in the left pocket,
a hanky often signals the wearer is a
top. For bottoms, the hanky is placed
in the right pocket. A light-blue hanky
supposedly shows preference for oral
sex, and last but not least, a dark-blue
hanky means the wearer is looking for
anal action.

shrimping, v.

the act of sucking toes during sexual play; *American*

> They say **shrimping** is the most common sexual fanstasy after the threesome.

shuck the oyster, v.

to have sex; *American*

> They say that men with rough hands **shuck the best oysters**.

shysexual, n., adj.

someone who shows little or no interest in sex of any kind; *American*

> Poor Theodore isn't just shy, he's **shysexual**.

sick, adj., adj.

slang for cool; *American*

> If you think that's a **sick** monkey, look at this giant alligator—now that's ill.

sick, n.

puke; *British*

> When Patricia missed the toilet, she left **sick** all over the bathroom floor.

> When Patricia missed the toilet, she left **puke** all over the bathroom floor.

sick as a parrot, adj.
very disappointed, crushed; *British*

> Maria was **sick as a parrot** when her boyfriend told her he had rented *Beaches* but instead rented Takashi Miike's *Visitor Q.*

> Maria was **very disappointed** when her boyfriend told her he had rented *Beaches* but instead rented Takashi Miike's *Visitor Q.*

sideways smile, n.
an ass crack; *American*

> She bent over in these really low cut jeans and revealed her **sideways smile** to the whole place.

siphon the python, v.
to pee; *British*

> I'm going to **siphon the python** in the alleyway over there because it's closer than the bathroom in the restaurant.

> I'm going to **pee** in the alleyway over there because it's closer than the bathroom in the restaurant.

size queen, n.
one who places extreme importance on her or his partner's penis size; *American*

> Don't tell a **size queen** that you've got a big dick unless you're ready to pull down your drawers and prove it.

skank, n.

slut; reggae dance; *American*

> When that **skank** hit on my husband, I spilled my cosmo all over her Jimmy Choos.

> If that's not the **skank** calling the whore a slut.
> —*One Tree Hill*

skanky, adj.

dirty; slutty; *American*

> **Skanky** is as **skanky** does.

> What, am I not **skanky** enough for you, you want me to hike up my fucking skirt?
> —*Knocked Up*

skeet, v.

to ejaculate; *American*

> It can be very hard to **skeet** when you're drunk off your ass.

skeevy, adj.

creepy; *American*

> When that **skeevy** guy kept hitting on Pamela, she had her boyfriend the bouncer toss him out of the bar and onto the street.

> There's times to be real, and there's times to be phony. That's right, I said it, phony! You think I'm this nice in real life? Fuck that, son! That's just 'cause I'm on TV. I'd pull my balls out right now . . . **skeet skeet skeet skeet**!
> —*Chappelle's Show*

skeeza, n.

promiscuous woman; *American*

> If you're going to have sex with that **skeeza**, you better make sure you wear some protection.

skid mark, n.
shit stain on underwear; *American*

> Underwear Rule #1: If you're leaving **skid marks**, wash your own underwear.

> Why dincha just piss off, Fischer? Ya dotty wee **skid mark**!
> —*Rushmore*

skin flute, n.
penis; *American*

> I once fucked a clarinetist and boy, his **skin flute** was the highlight of my one-night stands.

skin up, v.
to roll a joint; *British*

> I'm way too high to **skin up**, so you do it, you lazy prick.

> I'm way too high to **roll this joint**, so you do it, you lazy prick.

skins, n.
rolling papers; *British*

> Pass me the **skins** and I'll make us a joint, so we can properly watch *Pineapple Express*.

> Pass me the **rolling papers** and I'll make us a joint, so we can properly watch *Pineapple Express*.

skive off, v.
to cut class; *British*

> Screw geometry class—let's **skive off** and smoke some joints in the car park.

> Screw geometry class—let's **cut class** and smoke some joints in the parking lot.

skunk, n.
poor quality marijuana; *American*

> **Skunk** is junk, don't waste your hard-earned allowance on it.

slag, n.
slut; *British*

> Ian's such a shysexual even the **slags** won't chat him up.

> Ian's such a shysexual even the **sluts** won't talk to him.

slag someone off, v.
to bad mouth someone; *British*

> That bitch keeps **slagging me off**, so I started a rumor that she was a hermaphrodite and she still had both a gun and a holster.

> That bitch keeps **bad mouthing me**, so I started a rumor that she was a hermaphrodite and she still had both a gun and a holster.

slap magnet, n.

slut; *American*

> Patricia may wear short skirts and fishnets, but she's no **slap magnet**.

slaphead, n.

bald person; *British*

> Bruce Willis, now that's one fit **slaphead**!
>
> Bruce Willis, now that's one hot **bald guy**!

slapper, n.

slut, ho; *British*

> Mate, I'm only your friend because your sister is a **slapper** and I want to shag her.
>
> Dude, I'm only your friend because your sister is a **slut** and I want to fuck her.

slashers, n.

testicles; *American*

> Urban legend has it that the bigger the **slashers**, the higher the IQ, which is why my dream fuck is Albert Einstein.

Sloane Ranger, n.
snob; *British*

That art exhibit was full of **Sloane Rangers** drinking champers, but the joke was on them because there wasn't any cheese and crackers.

That art exhibit was full of **snobs** drinking champagne, but the joke was on them because there wasn't any cheese and crackers.

Lone Rangers with Attitude
Sloane Rangers get their name from London's Sloane Square, located in the decidedly posh part of town most of them live in. Also refers to those well-paid individuals who work in the area. Rhymes with Lone Ranger . . . get it?

slob on someone's knob, v.
to give oral sex to a man; *British*

In his dreams, Jack's girlfriend is always **slobbing on his knob**.

In his dreams, Jack's girlfriend is always **blowing him**.

sloppy seconds, n.
the act of having sex with someone after that person has just had sex; *American*

If you're going to have **sloppy seconds** with someone, you should ask that person to shower first. Or not, if you have a sweat fetish.

So what's up? You got a friend for Silent Bob, or are you just gonna do us both? If so, I'm first. I hate **sloppy seconds**.
—*Dogma*

slore, n.
neologism combining "slut" and "whore"; *American*

Where does a **slore** draw the line between prick-tease and prick?

slump buster, n.
often an unattractive person used to break one's lack of recent sexual activity; *American*

> It's been six months since Theresa broke up with me—I just need to go out and find a **slump buster** to get back in the swing of things.

slurry bucket, n.
any orifice in which a hand may be inserted; *American*

> She wanted me to fit my whole hand into the **slurry bucket** between her legs.

slut, n.
promiscuous woman; *American*

> Ooh la la! Marie sees every business trip to Paris as a chance to be a **slut** with style.

> You total **slut**, you have a crush on him. You're defending him, you love him, you wanna have, like, ten thousand of his babies.
> —*American Beauty*

smack and jack, n.
the act of two men kissing while masturbating each other; *American*

> Our sex life has gotten so vanilla—we always start with a little **smack and jack** before moving on to a double header.

SMD, interj.
acronym for suck my dick; *American*

> You don't want to go to the prom with me? **SMD**, bitch!

smegma, n.
white creamy fluid that gathers under the foreskin; *American*

> There's no way I'm sucking you off until you wipe that nasty **smegma** off your acorn.

smelly bridge, n.
perineum; *American*

> When her tongue hit my **smelly bridge**, I shivered with pleasure but wished for her sake I'd showered earlier.

smexy, adj.
smart and sexy; *American*

> Librarians are the **smexiest** ladies around.

smiling like a donut, v.
opening one's mouth wide to perform oral sex on a man; *American*

> She **smiled like a donut**, but she really didn't have to because Harry had a really small dick.

smiling like a fish, v.
opening one's mouth to perform oral sex; *American*

> After a long night of **smiling like a fish**, our jaws were sore—but our privates were happy.

smurf, n.
cigar dipped in embalming fluid; *American*

> Smoke enough **smurfs** and you'll start hallucinating.

snarfing, n.
the act of licking around an anus; *American*

> **Snarfing**, rimming, call it what you'd like, but just remember to brush your teeth afterward.

snatch, n.
vagina; *American*

> That loser Larry is on the prowl for **snatch** every night—and every night he comes home empty-snatched.

> With grevious dispatch, I must get to that latch and unlock her **snatch**.
> —*Everything You Always Wanted To Know About Sex*

snipped, adj.
sterile due to a vasectomy; *American*

> You can go bareback with no risk, ladies—I'm **snipped**.

snow bunny, n.
white woman who socializes only with black men; *American*

> Forget about setting your cracker roommate up with Sandra; she's a **snow bunny**.

snowball, v.

to ejaculate in someone's mouth then that person spits the cum into either the original person's or someone else's mouth; *American*

I came in my girlfriend's mouth, and as a prank, she kissed my roommate and **snowballed** him. He subsequently never looked at either one of us the same way again.

After he gets a blowjob, he likes to have it spit back into his mouth while kissing—it's called **snowballing**.
—*Clerks*

SOB, n.

acronym for son-of-a-bitch; *American*

You can tell that **SOB** he's got until Friday afternoon to pay me back or he'll lose a pinky.

sod, n.

dummy; idiot; *British*

Poor **sod**. His wife left him for a lawyer who makes the big bucks.

Poor **dummy**. His wife left him for a lawyer who makes the big bucks.

sod off!, interj.

fuck off; get lost; *British*

Sod off! The thought of spending the night with your hairy ball sack between my legs makes me ill.

Fuck off! The thought of spending the night with your hairy ball sack between my legs makes me sick.

soft lad, n.

softie (negative); *British*

> If you're a greenhorn and a **soft lad** on *Deadliest Catch*, you are more than likely going to be rightfully berated and probably eventually fired.

> If you're a greenhorn and a **softie** on *Deadliest Catch*, you are more than likely going to be rightfully berated and probably eventually fired.

spank the monkey, v.

to masturbate; *American*

> Clarence couldn't answer the phone because he was **spanking the monkey**.

> In a world gone mad, we will not **spank the monkey**, but the monkey will spank us.
> —*Jay and Silent Bob Strike Back*

spare, adj.

at wits end, crazy; *British*

> Charlie's parents went **spare** when they found out he was dropping acid, but then mellowed out by smoking from their cannabis supply.

> Charlie's parents went **crazy** when they found out he was dropping acid, but then mellowed out by smoking from their cannabis supply.

spaz, n.

crazy or unpredictable person; *American*

> You're such a **spaz**— can't you just act normal for a minute?

> Oh, I don't get wild. Wild on me equals **spaz**.
> —*Buffy the Vampire Slayer*

spend a penny, v.
to go to the bathroom; *British*

> Do you need to **spend a penny** before we set off because last time you pissed yourself?

> Do you need **to go to the bathroom** before we leave because last time you pissed yourself?

spill one's seed, v.
to have sex; *American*

> Condoms aren't foolproof, and somehow Joe managed to **spill his seed**, literally.

spit fuck, v.
to have sexual intercourse with only saliva as lubricant; *American*

> Even in his most romantic moments, Charles never took the time for proper foreplay and proceeded directly from a quick kiss to a **spit fuck**.

spitroast, n.
double penetration by mouth and either vagina or anus; *American*

> During the **spitroast** last night, we should've had a cleaning woman there to mop up the chick's dripping juices.

spitting game, v.
attempting to seduce someone; *American*

> Daryl has been **spitting game** with that hot blonde for ten minutes and she still hasn't given him her digits.

splash out on something, v.
to spend a lot of money on something; *British*

> We **splashed out on** Manolo Blahnik pumps and then the recession hit. Unfortunately, you can't eat shoes.

> We **spent a lot of money on** Manolo Blahnik pumps and then the recession hit. Unfortunately, you can't eat shoes.

spliff, n.
marijuana cigarette; *American*

> I just scored some kiss-ass weed bro'—let's grab some beers and roll a **spliff** down at the lake.

> Well, you don't roll like, big rasta **spliff** joints, do you? Your joints are like salad joints, not like a big, sloppy, bleeding cheeseburger-that-you-rip-into-kind-of-a-joint joint.
> —*Igby Goes Down*

splooge, n.
semen; *American*

> Dirk shot his **splooge** on my tramp stamp last night.

spotty, adj.
pimply; *British*

> Today's **spotty** teenager is tomorrow's Cameron Diaz.

> Today's **pimply** teenager is tomorrow's Cameron Diaz.

spread eagle, n., v.
sexual position in which a woman's legs are spread wide in a V shape; *American*

> I came home early from school, and there my mom was, **spread eagle** with the mailman between her legs.

spunk, n.
semen; *American*

To keep her skin soft, Rosemary carefully applies old **spunk** she drains from her roommate's used condoms each night.

Simon: It's *your* **spunk**!
Neil: But it's *your* car!
Simon: What . . . so if I **spunked** in your face it would be yours?
—*The Inbetweeners*

spunk bucket, n.
vagina; slut; *American*

Call me a clean freak, but after every two johns, I like to empty my **spunk bucket**.

squiffy, adj.
slightly drunk; *British*

When Deloris gets **squiffy**, she gets very horny—so her husband always keeps champagne on ice.

When Deloris gets **slightly drunk**, she gets very horny—so her husband always keeps champagne on ice.

squits, n.
diarrhea; *British*

The **squits** that I just unleashed probably demolished the toilet in that restaurant.

The **diarrhea** that I just unleashed probably demolished the toilet in that restaurant.

stag do, n.
bachelor party; *British*

> At Mitch's **stag do**, the boys shaved his bollocks and wrote "We Were Here" on them.

> At Mitch's **bachelor party**, the boys shaved his balls and wrote "We Were Here" on them.

stalk, n.
erect penis; *Irish*

> Two pints later and Patrick's **stalk** had turned to a whiskey dick.

> Two pints later and Patrick's **hard-on** had turned to a limp biscuit.

stanky, adj.
stinky, smelly; *American*

> After ten days stuck at home in his studio with the stomach flu, Rob's apartment was beyond **stanky**.

stapes, n.
hairy armpits; *Irish*

> Take a look at the **stapes** on that boiler, will you?

> Take a look at the **hairy armpits** on that dog, will you?

starfish, n.
anus, asshole; *American*

> As I was banging her from behind and looking down at her **starfish**, all I could wonder was if she was into anal.

starfucker, n.

fan obsessed with having sexual intercourse with celebrities; *American*

> LA is chock-a-block with wannabe actresses and **starfuckers**—sometimes it's hard to tell who's who.

STD, n.

a sexually transmitted disease; *American*

> You're saying that his brain could have been cooked by an **STD**?
> —*Fringe*

> I went to this club that was so sketchy that I wouldn't have been surprised if I contracted an **STD** just by being in proximity of all those douchebags and sluts.

Steely Dan, n.

erection; *American*

> You know that guy who drives the old orange VW bus around town? He offered me a ride the other day and his **Steely Dan** was really distracting.

steeple, n.

penis; *American*

> As a deeply religious man, Freddie always said a prayer to avoid premature ejaculation before shoving his **steeple** in his wife's holy place.

Stevie girl, n.

a loud, annoying drunk girl who pronounces "Stevie" with a high-pitched squeal to gain attention; an attention whore; *American*

> The other night Cassandra turned into the ultimate **Stevie girl** and wouldn't shut up about her "crazy drinking stories."

sticky wicket, n.

sticky situation; *British*

> The moment he mentioned his other girlfriend, Charles knew he was batting from a **sticky wicket**.

> The moment he mentioned his other girlfriend, Charles knew he was in a **sticky situation**.

stiffie, n.

erection; *American*

> When I sat on Santa's lap, he called out Ho Ho Ho, and I could feel his **stiffie**.

> I don't know about the plot but I'm gettin a **stiffie**.
> —*Scream 2*

stir up the yogurt, v.

to copulate; *American*

> For breakfast, I prefer **stirring up the yogurt**—I like mine with big nuts and sticky honey.

stitch up, v.

to con; *British*

> Chester **stitched** me **up** and left me with the bill for the brothel.

> Chester **conned** me and left me with the bill for the brothel.

stonker, n.

huge thing; *British*

> My lord! Your knob is a **stonker**—it deserves to have its own zip code.

> My lord! Your knob is a **huge thing**—it deserves to have its own zip code.

storm the cotton gin, v.

to have sex; *American*

> After a couple of martinis, **storming the cotton gin** is the only thing on my mind.

straight, adj.

heterosexual; *American*

> Are there any **straight** single guys left in San Francisco?

> Let's make a law that gay people can have birthdays, but **straight** people get more cake—you know, to send the right message to kids.
> —*Bill Maher*

stranger, n.

the act of sitting on one's hand to make it numb then jerking off so it feels like someone else is doing it; *American*

> I feel it's safer to do the **stranger** instead of picking up an actual stranger at a bar to do the same thing.

streetmeat, n.

naïve person who can't survive on the streets; *American*

> Shawna left home with only twenty bucks and ten condoms hoping to make some easy money, but I fear she's **streetmeat**.

stroppy, adj.

irritating, annoying; *British*

> Georgina received a **stroppy** text from her boyfriend about his Asian fetish last night. Georgina is not Asian.

> Georgina received an **annoying** text from her boyfriend about his Asian fetish last night. Georgina is not Asian.

strumpet, n.
promiscuous woman; *American*

> You slept with my brother? Out **strumpet**, and take your things with you!

stubby, n.
small glass or bottle of beer; *Australian*

> I'll jam that **stubby** up your ass if you order another one out of manly principle.

> I'll jam that **small glass of beer** up your ass if you order another one out of manly principle.

stud muffin, n.
attractive, fashionable guy who gets a lot of female attention, similar to pimp-daddy; *American*

> With his hot bod and square jaw, Brad Pitt is a total **stud muffin**.

stuff, v.
to have sex; *British*

> If you're lucky, you can get **stuffed** in London without eating a bite.

> If you're lucky, you can **have sex** in London without eating a bite.

subbie, n.
submissive role in a dominant/submissive relationship; *American*

> If Alice wasn't into being the **subbie** in our relationship, I wouldn't be able to get it up.

succubus, n.

a demon who takes the form of a woman to have sex with men while they sleep; a needy, insecure girlfriend or wife who sucks away her significant other's soul and life; *American*

Oh, thanks for the newsflash, Tom Brokaw! What happened with Chef? Did you tell him she's a **succubus**?
—*South Park*

After Lonnie married Margaret, we basically never saw him again because his **succubus** of a wife would scream at him if he even looked at another woman, much less was friends with ladies.

....

suck, v.

to be crappy; *American*

My ex **sucked** at baseball. He was always more of a hockey man.

What's the difference between a Democrat and a Republican? A Democrat blows, a Republican **sucks**!
—*Lewis Black*

suck a fuck, v.

to tell someone to "fuck off"; sucking the after results of sex; *American*

If you're not going to let me borrow your car so I can take your sister out for a nice time then destroy her, you can go **suck a fuck**.

Elizabeth: Did you just call me a fuckass? You can go **suck a fuck**. Donnie: Oh, please, tell me Elizabeth, how exactly does one **suck a fuck**?
—*Donnie Darko*

suck face, v.

to French kiss; *American*

> Despite **sucking face** for a half hour, he couldn't get his girlfriend to move on to second base.

suck someone off, v.

to perform fellatio on someone; *American*

> When Christine met Angelo at the wedding reception, by the third martini they were under the table **sucking each other off**. Thank God for those long tablecloths.

suck up, v.

to appease; *American*

> Because he sucks at his job, Jack tries to make up for it when he **sucks up** to his boss.

suckalicious, adj.

extremely attractive, meriting sucking; *American*

> Pamela's titties are **suckalicious**!

sugar daddy, n.

well-off older man who dates younger partners; *American*

> There's no fool like an old **sugar daddy**.

You mean a **sugar daddy**, who tries to teach me how to act? I read books. I want to know everything. Doesn't it make sense to have plans?
—*Once Upon a Time in America*

sugar lumps, n.
small breasts; *American*

> Tony had a thing for girls with **sugar lumps**, so he loved Martha and her triple As.

sugar momma, n.
well-off older woman who dates younger partners; *American*

> That **sugar momma** paid for my meal, then made me her meal in bed.

sugared almond, n.
clitoris; *American*

> While sucking her **sugared almond**, he slowly slid a finger, then two, into her pussy.

sundries, n.
freebies; *Australian*

> Our local take-away always gives us loads of **sundries** like free starters and drinks because our friend fucked the owner and she doesn't want anybody to know about it.

> Our local take-out always gives us lots of **freebies** like free appetizers and drinks because our friend fucked the owner and she doesn't want anybody to know about it.

surfing the crimson wave, v.

to be menstruating; *American*

> With her nasty commentary at my yearly review, I would swear my boss is **surfing the crimson wave**.

swamp ass, n.

sweaty buttocks; *American*

> There's nothing hotter than creaming your corn on a tight little **swamp ass** at the gym after a serious workout.

swan sauce, n.

sweat that accumulates around a woman's vagina in the heat; *American*

> At the gym, Jerry goes for the girls who work out the hardest—he loves hard bodies swimming in **swan sauce**.

to swap gravies, v.

to have sex; *American*

> You could say I wasn't in the mood for turkey last Thanksgiving after I caught my Aunt Bertha and Uncle Sam **swapping gravies**.

sweater meat, n.

breasts visible under a sweater; *American*

> In the 1950s, my grandmother liked to show off her **sweater meat** with a tight cardigan.

sweet, adj.
great, cool; *American*

> Your grandpa got you a **sweet** convertible for your sixteenth birthday? Sick!

sweet as a nut, adj.
fine, just great; *British*

> How am I? Well, I just busted a nut, so I am **sweet as a nut**.

> How am I? Well, I just ejaculated, so I am **just great**.

switch hitter, n.
bisexual; *American*

> When Sam found out that his wife Kate was a **switch hitter**, he invited his lipstick-lesbian secretary over for dinner.

swoops, n.
bangs from one side of the forehead that go across the forehead and cover one eye; *American*

> Look at the girl with the **swoops** over there—she's like a hot cyclops!

sword, n.
penis; *American*

> The gay knights at Camelot fought all their battles with big **swords**.

Sybian, n.

brand of women's masturbation apparatus similar to a mounted, vibrating dildo; *American*

> If only I had an extra grand lying around, I'd finally buy that custom **Sybian** I have my heart set on.

symphorophilia, n.

sexual disorder in which pleasure is stimulated by watching accidents or injuries; *American*

> The movie *Crash*, directed by David Cronenberg and released in 1996, was one of the first Hollywood films to show **symphorophilia** in action.

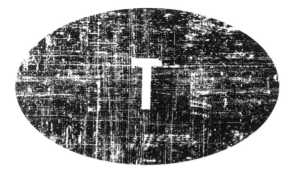

tab, n.

cigarette; *British*

> She usually likes to smoke a **tab** before, during, and after we have sex—my kind of woman.

> She usually likes to smoke a **cigarette** before, during, and after we have sex—my kind of woman.

table-ender, n.

sexual intercourse on a table; *American*

> My biggest fantasy is a **table-ender** threesome with Emeril Lagasse and Jamie Oliver.

taco, n.

pussy; *American*

> Pink tacos, fish tacos, whatever—there's no **taco** Marty won't eat.

tadge, n.
penis; *British*

For twenty quid, I'll shag you, but there's no way your wrinkled old **tadge** is ending up in my mouth.

For twenty pounds, I'll screw you, but there's no way your wrinkled old **dick** is ending up in my mouth.

tadpole, n.
man that dates much older women; *American*

When my mom turned fifty, she dumped her boring, balding boyfriend and snagged herself a **tadpole**.

taint, n.
perineum; *American*

It ain't pussy and it ain't ass, but damn, does **taint** taste good.

I think she wants me to rub olive oil on your **taint**.
—*Baby Mama*

to take a ride on the Hershey Highway, v.
to have anal sex; *American*

I'm so excited for my date tonight! He said he'd pick me up in his convertible and after dinner we'd **take a ride on the Hershey Highway**.

take the mickey out of someone, v.

to mock someone; to pull someone's leg; *British*

If John starts to **take the mickey out of you**, just tell him how awful his mother was in bed last night.

If John starts to **mock you**, just tell him how awful his mother was in bed last night.

'Cause she knows we'd **take the mickey out of her** if she did.
—*Harry Potter and the Goblet of Fire*

take the piss, v.

to make fun; *British*

If you can't handle when we **take the piss** of you, you should learn to take it as well as you give it out.

If you can't handle when we **make fun** of you, you should learn to take it as well as you give it out.

Are you **taking the piss**?
—*Snatch*

take the veil, v.

when a gay man marries a woman; *American*

Harold **took the veil** for his parents' sake, but divorced and moved in with a twinkie the minute they kicked the bucket.

Nuns are said to take the veil when taking their religious vows, as if they were marrying God. The vow of poverty may not be insufferable, but the vow of chastity is only for the truly brave.

talk shit, v.

to go talk nonsense; *American*

The boss is always **talking shit** while we do all the real work.

Man, that's all we ever do is **talk shit**.
—*8 Mile*

talk to God on the big white telephone, v.
to vomit; *British*

> If you need to **talk with God on the big white telephone** when we get in my car, try to project your puke away from the side of my car.

> If you need to **puke** when we get in my car, try to project your puke away from the side of my car.

tallywhacker, n.
dick; *American*

> It doesn't make you a whore, but I'm sure you've got twice as many **tallywhackers** in your mouth as I have.

tap ass, v.
to have sex; *American*

> My Spanish lover insisted on tapas before **tapping ass**—he said he couldn't concentrate on an empty stomach.

> What would JFK do? You know he'd **tap** that **ass**.
> —*The Girl Next Door*

tart, n.
slut; *British*

> After we broke up, my ex still rang me twice a week for some nookie. What a **tart**!

> After we broke up, my ex still called me twice a week for some nookie. What a **slut**!

> A gourmet who thinks of calories is like a **tart** who looks at her watch.
> —*James Beard*

tea bag, v.

to put one's testicles into someone's mouth or slap them on someone's face, sometimes when unexpected; *American*

Don't leave your Uncle T-Bag hanging.
—*Arrested Development*

> We decided to **tea bag** Martin to get back at him for drinking all of our whiskey.

team cream, n.

group sex; *American*

> When we won the varsity championship, the entire offense and half the cheerleading squad celebrated with a drunken **team cream**.

texthole, n.

a person who sends unpleasant or nasty text messages, often in inappropriate situations; *American*

> I paid almost twenty bucks to get into this damn movie and that **texthole** in front of me has been on his iPhone since the credits!

thai sticks, n.

marijuana soaked in hasish oil, often tied to bamboo sticks; *American*

> One time, I tried to impress this sexy pothead with **thai sticks**, but she ended up just smoking all my weed.

thatch, n.
pubic hair; hairy vagina; *British*

> Snatch with a **thatch**, that's what the girls called me in junior high school after just one shower in gym class.

> **Hairy** snatch, that's what the girls called me in junior high school after just one shower in gym class.

thick, adj.
dumb; *British*

> Mark the Mimbo is cute, but he's incredibly **thick**.

> Mark the Mimbo is cute, but he's incredibly **dumb**.

thicko, n.
dimwit; *British*

> Oi **thicko**, you usually should wait for the band to start playing before you start a mosh pit.

Oh, Mr **Thicko**, fancy not knowing that!
—*Blackadder Goes Forth*

> Hey **dimwit**, you usually should wait for the band to start playing before you start a mosh pit.

the three gets, n.
stands for "get home, get off, get out"; *American*

> Maureen thought that after their passionate lovemaking, Giovanni would cuddle her until the sun came up, but it was clearly a case of **the three gets**.

threequel, n.
third in a series; *American*

> The *Pirates of the Caribbean* **threequel** was nowhere near as good as the first two films.

> **DERIVATION:** This term comes from the words three + sequel.

thrombing, n.
a session of intense, aggressive sex; *American*

> We were both horny and pissed off, so I ripped her clothes off and gave her a hellacious **thrombing**.

throw a wobbly, v.
to throw a tantrum; *British*

> My boss **threw a wobbly** when he found out I'd quit. It was funny as fuck.

> My boss **threw a tantrum** when he found out I'd quit. It was funny as fuck.

thugby, n.
derogatory term for rugby implying all players and fans are thugs; *British*

> Go out for the **thugby** team? I might as well just get drunk and rowdy with friends at home.

tiger stripes, n.
stretch marks; *American*

> After two kids, the **tiger stripes** on Laila's hips could scare the bejesus out of a man.

tight ass, n.

cheap or uptight person; also, nice, firm buttocks; *American*

> Don't be such a **tight ass**—let me go down on you.

I'm gonna grab you by your Brooks Brothers PJs, and then I'm gonna take your brand new BMW, and cram it up your **tight ass**!
—*Caddyshack II*

TILF, n.

acronym for "Teacher I'd Like to Fuck"; *American*

> I wasn't a big fan of older men in high school, but Mr Boyer was definitely a **TILF**.

tit for tat, interj.

an expression meaning, roughly, "quid pro quo"; *American*

> **Tit for tat** is the basis upon which all mutual pleasure should be founded—one orgasm at a time.

They say that life is **tit for tat**, and that's the way I live . . . so I deserve a lotta tat for what I've got to give.
—*Chicago*

tits, n.

breasts; *American*

> There's nothing like a pair of babelicious **tits** to distract the boys.

> **DERIVATION:** Tit is one of the many variations of *teat,* which comes to us from the Old English *titt,* meaning breast. Take that into your mouth and suck it.

I do have big **tits**. Always had 'em—pushed 'em up, whacked 'em around. Why not make fun of 'em? I've made a fortune with 'em.
—*Dolly Parton*

titty bar, n.

a strip club; *American*

> My friends and I went to the **titty bar**, but left because too many of the strippers had beef curtains.

titty fuck, v.

to rub one's penis between a woman's breasts; *American*

> Nelly may be a goody-two-shoes virgin, but she still lets me **titty fuck** her.

> Fuck the phones, Lloyd! Unless Carmen Electra calls for an emergency **titty fuck**, don't answer!
> —*Entourage*

todger, n.

penis; *British*

> Does that bloke have a third leg? Oh, wait, it's just his giant **todger**.

> Does that dude have a third leg? Oh, wait, it's just his giant **penis**.

> Personally, I'd recommend you get a hold of a cocker spaniel, tie your suspect down on a chair with a potty on his head, then pop his **todger** between two floury buns and shout "Dinner time, Fido!"
> —*Blackadder Goes Forth*

toe cleavage, n.

the part of the toes exposed in low-cut shoes, usually high heels; *American*

> There's nothing like a little **toe cleavage** to make a foot fetishist's day.

toe rag, n.
loser, worthless; *British*

> Stop being a little **toe rag** and jam those dollar bills in that stripper's G-string like you mean it.

> Stop being a little **loser** and jam those dollar bills in that stripper's G-string like you mean it.

toke, v.
to take a hit of cannabis smoke; *American*

> I usually **toke** up right before my girlfriend gets home from work and starts complaining about her day.

tomtit, n.
shit; *British*

> I slipped in some **tomtit** but luckily, I fell on my blow-up sex doll.

> I slipped in some **dog shit** but luckily, I fell on my blow-up sex doll.

top, n.
gay man who prefers dominating, i.e. being on top; *American*

> Nothing can top a **top** who tops off, filling me to the brim with warm, salty cum.

tosser
jerk; *British*

> I will ram my car into that **tosser** who cut me off.

> I will ram my car into that **jerk** who cut me off.

> Oh leave it out! You **tossers**! You had one job to do!
> —*Ocean's Eleven*

- -

tough shit, interj.
too bad; *American*

> So you don't like your mother's chicken bake? **Tough shit** kid, eat up.

- -

tough titties, interj.
an expression meaning, roughly, tough shit; *American*

> Tara told Tom **tough titties** when he begged her forgiveness for feeling up her twin sister's tits on New Year's Eve.

> **DERIVATION:** We may have the pioneers to thank for this charming expression. The story is that on the long trek west on the wagon trail, tired moms gave their teething babies stale bread soaked in milk for their sore gums. They called them tough titties.

> How would you like to die? Hmm? Broken neck? Broken back? How's about I start with your arm . . . then your leg . . . then your other arm . . . then your ribcage . . . finishing off with a spinning roundhouse kick to the head, breaking your neck. Hmm? Sounds good? Works for me. And if it doesn't work for you, then **tough titties**.
> —*The Killing Zone*

- -

town bike, n.
town whore; *American*

> Lauren was well known as the **town bike** by everybody.

trade junk, v.

to have sex without commitment; *American*

> When you want to **trade junk**, just call a fuck buddy.

tradesman's entrance, n.

anus, rear door; *British*

> If a girl has just had Mexican food, you should avoid going up her **tradesman's entrance**.
>
> If a girl has just had Mexican food, you should avoid going up her **ass**.

> So I tell the swamp donkey to sock it before I give her a trunky in the **tradesman's entrance** and have her lick me yarbles!
> —*EuroTrip*

trainspotter, n.

nerd, geek; *British*

> The **trainspotter** spent all of his spare time nitpicking the inaccuracies in *Star Wars* and dreaming of having sex with Princess Leia.
>
> The **geek** spent all of his spare time nitpicking the inaccuracies in *Star Wars* and dreaming of having sex with Princess Leia.

tramp, n.

promiscuous woman; *American*

> Margaret may be fifty but she still dresses like a two-bit **tramp**.

> A man can sleep around, no questions asked, but if a woman makes nineteen or twenty mistakes, she's a **tramp**.
> —*Joan Rivers*

tramp stamp, n.

tattoo placed on a woman's lower
back; *American*

> One woman's **tramp stamp** is
> another woman's declaration of
> undying love—until she dumps the
> lying SOB and is stuck with his name
> on her ass.

Ah, the **tramp stamp**. My
bread and butter. So I'm
guessing that the real story
involves a bad breakup and
some booze? Unless that's a
gang tattoo, in which case I
think it's time to find a new
gang.
—*How I Met Your Mother*

tranny, n.

transsexual or transvestite;
American

> When Barry took Barbie to
> bed, he was surprised to find
> out she was a **tranny**; Barry
> doesn't like surprises.

Charlie: Take a look at this
picture. What do you see?
Mac: I see two **trannies**
shooting at each other.
Charlie: No, dude. They're
dueling, okay? These
are lawyers settling an
argument by dueling it out.
—*It's Always Sunny in
Philadelphia*

treat someone like shit, v.

to treat someone badly; *American*

> Why don't you break up with Stan?
> He's got a tiny cock, and what's
> more, he **treats you like shit.**

trick, n.

prostitution session or client; *American*

> At ten $50 **tricks** a night, I can earn enough to pay for college tuition *and*
> the boob job I've always wanted.

the trots, n.

the runs; *British*

My girlfriend's mincemeat pie always gives me the **trots**, and after I've been in the bathroom for most of the night, she's never in the mood to have sex.

My girlfriend's mincemeat pie always gives me the **runs**, and after I've been in the bathroom for most of the night, she's never in the mood to have sex.

trouser department, n.

penis (for a man); *British*

My fiancé is a dear but he's seriously lacking in the **trouser department** and I have a dildo handy just in case he can't do the trick.

My fiancé is a dear but he's seriously lacking a **large penis** and I have a dildo handy just in case he can't do the trick.

trout pout, n.

collagen-filled lips; *American*

Meg Ryan used to be the hottie next door, but now with that **trout pout** she looks like she's always ready for a quick suckie suckie.

trucker bomb, n.

container or bottle filled with urine; *American*

The big rig driver next to us on the highway was weaving in and out for a few minutes. When we saw him launch that **trucker bomb** at those skanky hoes on the off ramp, we knew why.

trustafarian, n.
a neologism combining trust fund and Rastafarian; young adult with a trust fund that allows him or her the financial security to work at a low-paying service industry job or follow his or her dream of becoming an artist or musician, all the while living a hippie lifestyle; *American*

> Williamsburg? Five years ago, the place was super cool; now it's filled with **trustafarians** and wannabes.

tryke, n.
lesbian male to female transsexual; *American*

> Among the transsexual crowd, **trykes** are definitely the least common.

tufted mussel, n.
an unshaved pussy; *American*

> Shakti Sunshine was a bit of a hippy and didn't believe in shaving down there, so she had quite a **tufted mussel**.

turd-burglar, n.
homosexual man; *American*

> That famous Scientologist actor has nothing against homosexuals—in fact, some of his best friends are **turd-burglars.**

turkey slap, v.
the act of a man slapping his penis on his partner's face; *American*

> Speaking of Thanksgiving, don't you dare **turkey slap** me after I've had to spend an entire afternoon talking to your Aunt Bertha.

to turn tricks, v.

to prostitute oneself; *American*

When the amateur magician lost all his bar mitzvah gigs, he sadly turned to **turning tricks**.

Illusion, Michael. A **trick** is something a whore does for money.
—*Arrested Development*

turtlehead, n.

when a piece of feces begins to exit the anus, just before defecation; *American*

Why do guys always wait until the **turtlehead** is poking out before sitting down to take a shit? That must be the reason for those ubiquitous skid marks.

First things first: *Where's Your Shitter?* I've got a **turtlehead** poking out.
—*Austin Powers—The Spy Who Shagged Me*

twat, n.

vagina; *American*

There comes a time in every man's life when he needs to learn to tongue the **twat**. Good.

Why don't you shut up and fucking sing, you **twat**.
—*Sid and Nancy*

twatface, n.

jerk; *American*

Don't be such a **twatface**, Dad. Just give me your PIN number and ATM card and I'll just take out enough to pay for lunch, I swear.

twerk, v.
to have sex; *American*

> **Twerking** a twink is harder than you think.

twink, n.
young, thin gay man with little body hair; *American*

> My cousin is gay but isn't interested in **twinks**—he's more of a bear man.

twinkie, n.
a person of Asian descent who more closely resembles white stereotypes; *American*

> Ji Yeon may be Korean, but she talks like a valley girl—what a **twinkie**.
>
> **DERIVATION:** This term comes from the famed American snack food, the Twinkie.

Mmm Mmm Good

Twinkies, which are often mocked for their long shelf life, are oblong yellow cakes filled with creamy white filling. Hence, the Twinkie reference for Caucasian-acting Asian-Americans: yellow on the outside, white in the middle.

twinkie, n.
penis; *American*

> To keep your figure, lay off the cookies and eat a **twinkie** instead—sperm has only six calories a teaspoon!

> I'm gonna get a plastic surgeon, get the **twinkie** back in the wrapper.
> —*House M.D.*

to twix someone, v.
to insert two fingers into an anus; *American*

> **Twixing** Chantal left my fingers brown and sticky, just like the candy bar.

two dots and a dash, n.
penis and testicles; reference to Morse code; gay; *American*

> See that pre-op over there? She may have big tits but she's still got **two dots and a dash**.

two in the pink and one in the stink, n.
two fingers in a woman's vagina and another in her anus; *American*

> Clive has big hands, so pleasuring his girlfriend with **two in the pink and one in the stink** with one hand shouldn't be a problem.

twunt, n.
mean or stupid person; *American*

> Fuck you, you rotten old **twunt**!

> **DERIVATION:** Twunt is a combination of the words twat and cunt.

twurk, v.
when a woman rubs her buttocks on a man while dancing; *American*

> Did you see that crazy redhead **twurking** me? I'm hard as a rock now.

Tyke, n.
derogatory term for someone from Yorkshire; *British*

> That **Tyke** nicked my banger. I'll kill him.

> That **asshole** from Yorkshire stole my car. I'll kill him.

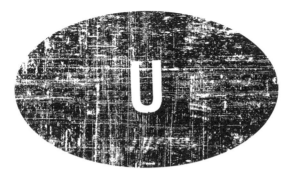

udder nonsense, n.

the act of fondling, groping, and sucking on breasts; *American*

> While the fucking was terrific, John equally enjoyed the **udder nonsense** with Brenda's perky tubes.

ultimate, n.

crack and marijuana joint; *American*

> An **ultimate** is the perfect joint for the crack whore who's looking for a laid-back Monday night.

ululate, v.

to make a guttural response to intense sexual pleasure; *American*

> Mary polished Ted's knob so exquisitely that in turn he yodeled, **ululated**, and invoked the name of several saints.

No, no, no, Tim. **Ululating** is a Middle Eastern custom expressing joy and sorrow.
—*Home Improvement*

umlauts, n.
breasts (from the German phonetic symbol of two dots over a vowel, usually U); *American*

> Appropriate given her Germanic lineage, Heidi had some nice **umlauts**.

unbutton the mutton, v.
to show one's penis; *American*

> To show his thanks for Isla helping him move, James **unbuttoned the mutton** during their drive to the shore and allowed Isla to admire and stroke the tire iron to attention.

Uncle Jim and the twins at attention, n.
the erect penis and testes; *American*

> By the time Tim got the flight attendant back to his apartment, there was clearly some local swelling in his pants, which upon removal, proved to be **Uncle Jim and the twins at attention**.

unclogging the drain, n.
female masturbation; *American*

> Paula let her husband know that she no longer needed his help in any respect: "Go out drinking with your buddies again, you son of a bitch, I'll be at home **unclogging the drain**, literally and metaphorically."

unshaggable, adj.
extremely unattractive; unfuckable; *British*

> Listen mate, it's your stag do. We want fit birds tonight, not the **unshaggable** tarts we usually wind up with.

> Listen buddy, it's your bachelor party. We want hotties tonight, not the **unfuckable** tarts we usually wind up with.

up a gum tree, adj.

confused; *Australian*

> Some think former President George W. Bush was genuinely evil, and others think he was just like Forrest Gump, **up a gum tree**.

> Some think former President George W. Bush was genuinely evil, and others think he was just like Forrest Gump, **confused**.

---

up against the stem, adj.

battling marijuana addiction; *American*

> My friend is **up against the stem** because his work now has drug tests. He should just quit his job, not his bong.

---

up for it, adj.

horny; *American*

> Judging from sticky juice running down her leg, I'd say Marion was really **up for it**.

---

up the duff, n.

pregnant, knocked up; *British*

> They've only been dating for a month, but Randy's girlfriend is already **up the duff**.

> They've only been dating for a month, but Randy's girlfriend is already **knocked up**.

> Maybe you didn't hear me, Doctor. Getting pregnant requires a certain physical element that I haven't had for a long time . . . I'm talking a *very* long time. I am a love-free zone, so it is utterly "impossible" that I be **up the duff**! What's your diagnosis "now"?
> —*Xena: Warrior Princess*

---

urophilia, n.

sexual disorder of fear or pleasure taken from acts involving urine; *American*

> **Urophilia** is more common than you'd think. Why, I once caught my own mother giving my dad a golden shower with a smile on her face—and his.

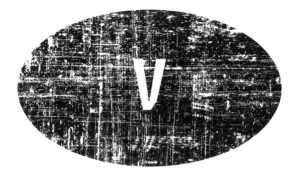

vag, n.

short for vagina; *American*

> Do you have anything for a yeast infection? My **vag** is killing me.

vagina, n.

female sex organ; *American*

> The **vagina** is the passageway from which all emerge and many spend the
> rest of their lives trying to get back into.
>
> **DERIVATION:** The word vagina comes from the Latin, meaning "sheath."

Synonyms of Vagina:

badly packed kebab	dick storage unit
bajingo	down there
beetle bonnet	downy bit
box	dugout
bucket hole	Elizabeth Regina
cake	fanny
cha cha	female parts
clam burger	flapjacks
clown pocket	flower
clunge	foo foo
cockholder	French drip sandwich
cooter	front bum
crawl space	fur burger
crumpet	furry goblet ›››

Synonyms of Vagina (continued)

guller buster
hair pie
hairy axe wound
hairy harmonica
ham wallet
holiest of holies
hoo-ha
joot
juicebox
kitty
lady bits
lady iPod dock
lotus blossom
love canal
love pudding
mailbox
map of Tazzie
meow-meow
Mimi
minge
minky
mongo
monkey box
mud flaps
muff
mushmellow
nanner
noonie

Octo-mom exit
pee hole
pleasure pit
poochie
poonanie
pound mound
powderbox
pudding pot
quim
salmon canyon
skin chimney
slit
sloppy fun pocket
sperm sponge
split knish
sweetness
tamale
tooshed
tulip
tunnel of love
twinkle
unit
whisker biscuit
wizard's sleeve
vagine (à la Borat)
Virginia
VJ
you-know-what

vaginal spaghetti, n.
a hairy vagina with dried menstrual blood; *American*

She didn't change her pad and had a case of **vaginal spaghetti** when the blood dried up on her bush.

vagitarian, n.
one who enjoys cunnilingus; *American*

> Lou was a man's man, and a steak was often tempting, but when push came to shove, he was a staunch **vagitarian**.

Vagoctopus, n.
a vagina, possibly of mythical origin, with tentacles; *American*

> Since my friend's wife is a succubus, I wouldn't be surprised if she had the mythical **Vagoctopus** that sucked his soul out with its tentacles of death.

to vaguebook, v.
to leave a vague update on Facebook with the hope of getting attention from curious friends; *American*

> I'm sick of Tom's **vaguebooking**—I mean, what kind of pathetic attempt for attention is "got the weirdest e-mail . . . " anyway?

va-jay-jay, n.
slang term for vagina; *American*

> Isla let her boyfriend know that her **va-jay-jay** was itchy, and if it was due to his infidelity with another, disease-ridden woman, Isla would cut off his dick, pan-fry it, and force feed it to him.

> O'Malley, stop looking at my **va-jay-jay**!
> —*Grey's Anatomy*

> **DERIVATION:** Popularized by Oprah, when she commented on her show: "I think **va-jay-jay** is a nice word, don't you?"

vanilla, adj.

conventional or boring sex;
American

> I've got to dump Harold
> one of these days—the sex
> used to be hot, but now it's
> so **vanilla**.

> **Vanilla**? I'm not **vanilla**. I've
> done lots of crazy things. I mean I
> got drunk and married in Vegas.
> —*Friends*

to veg out, v.

to relax, to zone-out; *American*

> We smoked a joint and spent
> the night **vegging out** and
> eating popcorn.

> Feel better? You call this feeling
> better? Or should I grab a bottle
> and **veg out** with you—avoid
> everything happening to me by
> just getting good and loaded?
> —*A Nightmare on Elm Street*

Venus with a penis, n.

pre-op male-to-female transsexual; transvestite;
American

> According to her classified ad, the tranny hooker was a
> buxom blonde. Unfortunately, a **Venus with a penis**
> doesn't come cheap and I settled on a slim, inexperienced
> Albanian hustler.

vertical smile, n.

slang term for vaginal lips; *American*

> He thought he'd stay a while after seeing her **vertical smile**.

voyeurism, n.

a sexual disorder that involves the need to observe others during sexual or private activity; *American*

> I don't mind my neighbor's **voyeurism** when he watches me undress through the open window, but watching me take a dump really crosses the line.

vulture capitalist, n.

businessperson who takes advantage of buying companies that are underpriced or having financial problems; *American*

> **Vulture capitalists** are just as bad as bankers; let's take them all out and shoot them.

wack off, v.

to jerk off; *American*

> My little brother **wacks off** every day before lunch at school.

> Miserable dead beat punk.
> Paid for his damn college.
> Sits around all day **wacking off**. Proud? My ASS.
> —*Freddie Got Fingered*

wack-ass, n.

crazy; *American*

> Get your **wack-ass**, motherfuckin' fro outta my face.

wacky backy, n.

pot, marijuana; *British*

> I can tell you've been smoking **wacky backy** because you've been dancing to Phish by yourself in the basement for the last hour.

> I can tell you've been smoking **pot** because you've been dancing to Phish by yourself in the basement for the last hour.

wah-wahs, n.

breasts; *American*

> Dolly Parton has the best **wah-wahs** in show business.

walk like Tarzan, talk like Jane, v.

when an attractive, muscular, "manly" gay man speaks in an effeminate manner; *American*

> That buff dude in the corner? He may **walk like Tarzan, but he talks like Jane**.

walk of shame, n.

when a person walks home wearing his or her clothes from yesterday (or someone else's clothes) and has a look on his or her face that says he or she made a huge mistake by having sex with someone the previous night; *American*

> After sleeping with the girl who he had previously told his friends was a succubus, Mark did the **walk of shame** the next morning.

> Hey look, it's my mom doing the **walk of shame** . . . out with the guy you met on a porn site?
> —*One Tree Hill*

wang, n.

dick; *American*

> She wanted to see if that douche bag's **wang** was as large as he said it was; however, when she saw how small it was, she laughed at him and left.

> It's time for me to boom-boom with the bridesmaids, Finch-fucker. 'Cause I'm gonna hang out with my **wang** out, and rock out with my cock out.
> —*American Wedding*

wanker, n.
jerk-off, asshole; *British*

> If you want to continue being a **wanker**, you should keep talking gobshite to that dude who looks like he could break you into two—oh, I'm sure he won't do it, just trust me.

> If you want to continue being an **asshole**, you should keep talking shit to that dude who looks like he could break you into two—oh, I'm sure he won't do it, just trust me.

wannabe, n.
someone who tries desperately to impress others with their style, but fails; *American*

> Last Christmas morning I found my dad wasted in a Santa suit with an empty bottle of whiskey next to him. Some **wannabe** St. Nick he turned out to be.

> Well, I'm tired of being a **wannabe** league bowler. I wanna be a league bowler!
> —*Dan Castellaneta*

war wound, n.
injury sustained during sexual congress; *American*

> Ted was a pantywaist draft dodger, but that didn't keep the sex maniac from sporting a bunch of **war wounds**.

Wassup?, interj.
slang term for "What's up?"; *American*

> Hey Jim, **wassup**? Been ages since we last talked.

Wassup Bud?

This expression was popularized by a Budweiser beer advertisement campaign, which ran from 1999–2002.

> Well, you can't kill me 'cause I'm already dead. And I talked to God, and she says, "Yo, **wassup**?" and she wants you to lose the gun.
> —*Empire Records*

wasted, adj.
inebriated; *American*

When Don's dog died, he got **wasted** and watched *Old Yeller* over and over again.

I never thought I was **wasted**, but I probably was.
—*Keith Richards*

to wax ass, v.
to have sexual intercourse; *American*

Sex with writers is always a let down. Stop waxing poetic and start **waxing ass**!

to waz, v.
pee; *British*

The water closet was destroyed during last night's party, so just **waz** on the lawn.

The bathroom was destroyed during last night's party, so just **pee** on the lawn.

wazzack, n.
idiot; *British*

If you don't sleep with that bird with the sleeve tattoos, you are a complete and utter **wazzack**.

If you don't sleep with that biddy with the sleeve tattoos, you are a complete and utter **idiot**.

wear a green carnation, v.
to be gay; *American*

On St. Patrick's Day, watch out for the leprechauns who **wear green carnations**.

DERIVATION: Green carnations were supposedly Oscar Wilde's code for homosexuality. Maybe he should have kept the carnations to a minimum; Wilde spent more than two years doing hard labor at Reading Gaol prison for the crime of homosexuality.

wear hinged heels, v.
to go to bed easily with someone; *American*

Sheryl **wears hinged heels** on hot dates.

DERIVATION: Hinged heels make it easier for a woman to flop onto her back.

to wear the bulky roll, n.
menstruating; *American*

Man, I am hornier than a virgin at a brothel. My fiancée has been **wearing the bulky roll** all week.

wedding tackle, n.
junk, dick; *British*

My Frank spends half his life showing off his **wedding tackle**. Heaven knows why—it's not much to write home about.

My Frank spends half his life showing off his **penis**. Heaven knows why—it's not much to write home about.

wedgie, n.
the act of forcefully grabbing someone by their underwear and attempting to lift them up; *American*

> Only assholes give people **wedgies**—and you should know.

You know, kids, a lot has changed since your old Uncle Joker's been away. New Gotham, new rules, even a new Batman. But now I'm tanned, I'm rested, and I'm ready to give this old town a **wedgie** again!
—*Batman Beyond: Return of the Joker*

weed, n.
marijuana; *American*

> Son, don't smoke too much **weed** or you'll grow up to be a loser like your father.

You know, don't get down on yourself: You got a great girl, you got a great job where you don't do anything, you get to **smoke weed** all day . . . I wish I had that. . . .
—*Pineapple Express*

weegie, n.
derogatory term for a person from Glasgow; *Scottish*

> Bloody hell, noisy **weegies** have invaded the hotel.

> Fuck, noisy **Glaswegians** have invaded the hotel.

DERIVATION: Weegie is short for Glaswegian.

well-hung, adj.
well-endowed man; *American*

> When I went to bed with Shawn, he apologized in advance that the rumors that he was **well-hung** were false.

I know, let's play the virgin milkmaid and the **well-hung** stable boy.
—*The Producers*

wet, adj.
effeminate; *British*

> Richard is so **wet**; his girlfriend broke up with him two weeks ago and he's still crying.

> Richard is so **effeminate**; his girlfriend broke up with him two weeks ago and he's still crying.

---

wet dream, n.
dream during which a man ejaculates unconsciously, often occurs during puberty; *American*

> Johnny had a **wet dream** and tried to hide the stained sheets from his mom. Sadly, she found out anyway and told their preacher.

> You're the only man I know who can screw up his own **wet dream**.
> —*Flashpoint*

---

wet willy, n.
sticking a finger wet with spit in someone's ear; *American*

> All the school kids tortured the new girl by giving her **wet willies**.

---

wewe, n.
a female ghost who has large breasts that are drooping; *British*

> Does anybody else see the **wewe** stripping over there?

> Does anybody else see the **large-breasted ghost** stripping over there?

---

whack off, v.
to masturbate; *American*

> Justin **whacks off** every night to an old 70s porno filled with hairy bushes.

> What are you gonna make me do? Whack a guy? Off a guy? **Whack off** a guy? 'Cause I'm married.
> —*Family Guy*

whale eye, n.
anus; *American*

> The great, unwashed **whale eye** is just another dirty asshole.

whale tail, n.
the exposed top part of a girl's thong, which mimics the shape of a whale's tail; *American*

> There's this girl at my work who wears these low cut jeans with a thong every day, so I can see her **whale tail** whenever she walks past my desk.

whatchamacallit, n.
thing you don't know the name for; *American*

> Can you hand me that, oh, now I forgot the name, that **whatchamacallit** over there with the stripes?

what's your beef?, interj.
what's your problem?; *American*

> **What's your beef,** dude? I didn't bang your girlfriend, I just kissed her.

whinge, v.
to whine, complain; *British*

> Stop **whinging** and make me a sandwich now.

> Stop **whining** and make me a sandwich now.

whip it out, v.

to show one's penis; *American*

> Mary questioned the size of Joseph's wang, so he **whipped it out** so she could measure it.

> There are only two rules in television: Don't swear and don't **whip it out**.
> —*The Simpsons*

whiskey dick, n.

the inevitable temporary erectile dysfunction associated with too much alcohol consumption; *American*

> We went back to my place, but after all I drank that night, I had a case of **whiskey dick**, so she left a bit unfulfilled.

whiskey shit, n.

the diarrhea that usually follows a night of drinking whiskey; *American*

> After my ten Jack and cokes last night, I woke up in the morning with a serious bout of **whiskey shit** that made me late for work.

white caps, n.

arrogant jerks who wear white hats, usually partially slanted, at clubs; *American*

> We should brawl with those **white caps** and take their birds.

white honey, n.

semen; *American*

> Honestly, I don't mind swallowing. Sweet **white honey** is delicious *and* nutritious, with mostly protein and only six calories per teaspoon.

whitebread, adj.
boring; unoriginal; *American*

> Jessica considers herself a worldy artist, but her paintings are so **whitebread**—in comparison, Thomas Kincade looks like Picasso.

to whizz one's tits off, v.
to get high as a kite (on speed, amphetamines); *British*

> Jumping Jimmy was **whizzing his tits off** and talking incoherently through his toothless mouth.

> Jumping Jimmy was **getting high as a kite** and talking incoherently through his toothless mouth.

whore, n.
prostitute; a woman who sleeps with many men; *American*

> Two fat **whores** in sweats work the street I live on.

DERIVATION: The word whore comes from the Middle English *hore*, meaning "adulterer."

> You can lead a **whore** to culture, but you can't make her think.
> —*Dorothy Parker*

whore around, v.
to have sex with many people; *American*

> Thomas? The way he **whores around**, I wouldn't touch his dick with a ten-foot pole.

wifebeater, n.

sleeveless undershirt worn by low-income level men; *American*

> I know it's crazy, but even a college-educated, progressive woman like me still finds something sexy about a guy with tattoos in a **wifebeater**.

> I have some kerchiefs and some undershirts . . . I hear some people call them **wifebeaters,** which I think is kind of funny.
> —*Six Feet Under*

wifey, n.

often derogatory term for one's wife; *American*

> Ah yes, **wifey** has a headache again. Surprise, surprise.

wild card, n.

the friend in the group who makes things exciting by a crazy act or acts; *American*

> Because I cut the brakes! **Wild card**, bitches! Yeeeee-haw!
> —*It's Always Sunny in Philadelphia*

> We were standing outside of a bar when a cop on a horse started telling us to leave, so our **wild card** said to her, "If I had a gun and a horse, I could be an asshole, too."

willy, n.

penis; *American*

> Stuart never forgot the one time he zipped up too quickly, lacerating his **willy**. He wore button-fly slacks for the rest of the decade.

> There is a lot of rubbish written about toilet humor—people saying it is childish and pretending it is beneath them—but there is no doubting the effectiveness of a really good **willy** gag.
> —*Adrian Edmondso*

windshield wipers, n.
breasts; *American*

> If I promise to wash your car, can I touch your **windshield wipers**?

wingman, n.
a guy who assists his friend with getting a hot girl, by occupying her less attractive friend; also, a person who talks up his friend to a hot girl or starts a conversation with her then passes her on to his friend; *American*

> My friend was a perfect **wingman** because he started talking to this hot biddy then passed her on to me; unfortunately, she thought Bear Grylls was better than Les Stroud, so I decided I didn't want to have sex with her anymore.

winking, v.
when a girl with no panties accidentally flashes her vagina to a room full of people; *American*

> Virginia jumped on me at the bar and fell over; unfortunately, she was wearing a skirt and no panties and **winked** at the whole room.

Winnebagos, n.
breasts; *American*

> Willie drove cross-country just to check out some amazing **Winnebagos** his e-mail pen pal had shown him online.

womyn, n.
militant feminist/lesbian spelling of woman; *American*

This chick at a bar was telling me about how men created the language so they've controlled it since the beginning of time, and I immediately asked, "Wait, do you spell woman, **w-o-m-y-n**?"

Y a Woman?

This spelling uses a 'y' as a reference to the Y male chromosome.

to wonk, v.
to masturbate; *British*

Ryan was caught **wonking** during homeroom and had to spend the afternoon in detention.

Ryan was caught **masturbating** during homeroom and had to spend the afternoon in detention.

woody, n.
erection; *American*

Woody's **woody** bulged in his jeans—and the women swooned.

woofter, n.
homosexual; *British*

I don't want to worry you, but I think your boyfriend may be a **woofter** because he always seems to want a dick in his mouth.

I don't want to worry you, but I think your boyfriend may be a **homosexual** because he always seems to want a dick in his mouth.

wopbabaloobops, n.
breasts; *American*

If only I had a bigger pair of **wopbabaloobops**, I wouldn't have to sing the blues.

WTF, interj.
acronym for "what the fuck"; expression used to describe a messed up situation; *American*

When Maxwell wanted me to shove a dildo up his ass and call him "Sally," I was like "**WTF**?"

Ever wonder why these words are flying? Maybe aliens in another galaxy will one day read this and think **WTF**?
—*Fanboys*

wylin', v.
acting crazy or out of control; *American*

I started **wylin'** out after a few too many shots of tequila, but then on the way home, I was puking out of my friend's car window. My parents are very proud of me.

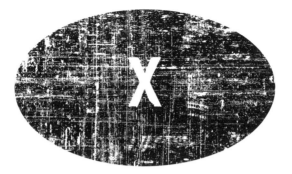

X, n.
the drug ecstasy; *American*

> I can't go to the rave without scoring some **X** first . . . otherwise I won't be able to dance all night.

XXX, n.
film rating given to the most sexually explicit movies by their makers; *American*

> This ain't no **XXX**! I have some dead wood here.

A Brief History of XXX

In November of 1968, bowing to pressure, mostly from religious corners, the Motion Picture Association of America (MPAA) put in place a voluntary rating system to alert would-be film goers of sexual themes, strong language, and violence. The now-familiar ratings of G, PG, R, and NC-17 (formerly X) were put in place. PG-13 was added later. When it comes to winning awards, screenwriters and filmmakers avoided X marking their spot, as that would sink all hope of a gold statue. But for the purveyors of golden showers on film, the porno industry, they not only embraced the X, but also beefed it up by putting it to the third power, XXX.

xanthodont, n.

a person with yellow teeth; *American*

> Anna said she really enjoyed fucking the carnival geek because, as she put it, he was hung like a garden hose about to burst, but had to break it off because he was a real **xanthodont**.

XDR, n.

cross-dresser; *American*

> When Harold told his wife he had to admit that he'd been seeing an **XDR** at night, she naively presumed he meant a new model down at the Ferrari showroom.

xenobiotic, n.

substance or item foreign to the body; *American*

> For the two lesbians happily in love, the twenty-three-inch black mambo dildo, their mate's fist, and occasionally the fine crystal stemware were not off limits to henhouse pleasure, but actual penises were strictly **xenobiotic**.

xenofuckic, adj.

afraid to be intimate with foreigners; *American*

> Suzy used to tag many of the women at the United Nations, but after a bad Lithuanian experience, she became **xenofuckic**, and now only eats Presbyterian pie.

xeric, adj.

dry, devoid of moisture and lubrication, as in the vaginal cavity; *American*

> Before there's any humpin' and bumpin,' we gotta get some KY Jelly for your **xeric** vagina.

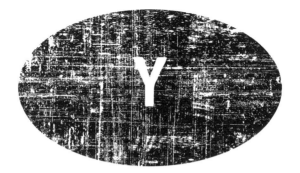

to yack, v.
to vomit; *American*

> I had some bad fish and wound up **yacking** for about half an hour and wasn't in the mood to give any blowjobs to my boyfriend.

> It can't be a dream! How can two people have the same dream? Okay, let's analyze this. In the middle of the night . . . did I get up . . . and **yack** in your sink?
> —*Weird Science*

yada yada yada, n.
meaning "blah blah blah" or "etc., etc., etc."; used to quickly skip sections or avoid going into details while telling a story; *American*

A Show about Yada
This term was popularized during the long-running comedy series *Seinfeld*.

> I thought she seemed like a conservative girl, we had dinner, went back to my place. **Yada yada yada**, I woke up chained to my bed with my body shaved and a burlap sack over my head.

to yang the wang, v.
to masturbate; *American*

> When he finishes his shift at his parents' Chinese restaurant, Lee spends most nights **yanging the wang** to porn movies with Mandarin subtitles.

yellow fever, n.
an interest and attraction toward Asian women; *American*

> Hal's got **yellow fever** so bad he has threatened to just move to Tokyo.

yestergay, adj., n.
former homosexual; *American*

> Seems like just yesterday my cousin Mervin was sucking cock and now look at that **yestergay**, dating an eighteen-year-old blonde.

yiffing, n.
pornography or sexual activity involving stuffed animals; *American*

> The best spot in my house for **yiffing** is my kid brother's bedroom. If only he knew where his beloved Sponge Bob had been!

youniverse, n.
the belief by a narcissist that the universe revolves around him or her; *American*

> If James realized aliens didn't really abduct and anoint him "Supreme Emperor of the Universe," his **youniverse** would come crashing down to reality.

yuppie, n.
young, urban professional; often drives a BMW or Mercedes and shows off material wealth; *American*

No offense, but most bankers are total BMW-driving **yuppie** assholes.

yupscale, adj.
describing a young professional who pretentiously shows off his or her wealth to gain attention; the word is a combination of "yuppie" and "upscale"; *American*

Rick really showed his superiority complex with his **yupscale** apartment, so I banged his wife and ejaculated all over his expensive furniture.

yupster, n.
a combination of yuppie and hipster; a hipster who, while remaining faithful to some hipster elements such as music or neighborhood, has embraced a yuppie career or lifestyle; *American*

When Matt gave up his gig as a DJ to concentrate more on his day job as an accountant, we knew that despite keeping his studio in Williamsburg, he had crossed the **yupster** line.

Yupsterville, n.
Williamsburg, Brooklyn is a neighborhood in New York City which has a high population of hipsters, vegetarian cafés, bars, organic grocery stores, and vintage clothing shops. The area, once a mecca of crime in the early 1980s, has seen one of the fastest gentrifications in urban history, and is now filled with so-called trustafarians, young adults with trust funds that allow them the financial security to work at low-paying service industry jobs or follow their dreams to be an artist or musician, while living a hipster lifestyle.

yutz, n.
an idiot, dolt; *American*

Don't be a **yutz**, she obviously likes you; now go over there and fuck her brains out.

It's a nightmare, we've been visited by the **Yutz** of Christmas Past.
—*The Golden Girls*

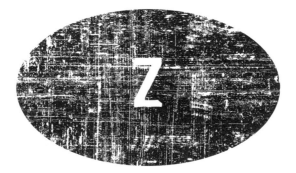

Z, n.

one ounce of heroin; *American*

> Just take a **Z** to get some ZZZs; you'll pass out immediately.

zab, n.

penis; *American*

> After inspecting the slight lesions on the underclassman's manhood, the hip campus doctor assured him the blood work was negative, then pulled out a balm and told him to "just put a dab on your **zab** each morning" for about a week.

zebra act, n.

an interracial couple; *American*

> These days, dating and marriage by two people of different races is generally accepted and not commented on, but my ancient Uncle Don still calls it a **zebra act**.

zeig heils
hemorrhoids; *British*

> The jogger rarely had running cramps, but in long road races often found himself with a humdinger case of **zeig heils**.

> The jogger rarely had running cramps, but in long road races often found himself with a humdinger case of **hemorrhoids**.

zeps, n.
large breasts (short for zeppelins); *American*

> Steve always went to that particular ticket clerk's window as she featured a near-perfect pair of **zeps**.

to zig zag, v.
to copulate; *American*

> The last time I **zig zagged,** I was so drunk I could hardly see straight.

zipper skipper, n.
a homosexual; *American*

> I thought he was just bored with my anecdote when he was staring down, but I'll be damned if that **zipper skipper** wasn't staring at my package!

zipper spark, v.
dry humping with your clothes on; *American*

> They were so hot for one another that they **zipper sparked** in the car in front of her parents' house until her dad came out to get her.

to zone out, v.

to daydream; to be lost in one's own world; *American*

> Sorry man, could you repeat that? I **zoned out** there for a minute.

People look at me and they get bored, people listen to me and they **zone out** . . . bored. "Who is that boring person?" they think. "I've never before met anyone so boring."
—*Happiness*

zoosexual, n.

person who prefers sexual activity with animals; *American*

> If you don't believe **zoosexuals** exist, you just have to watch some German porn or a Tiajuana donkey show.

RESOURCES

Miall, Anthony and David Milsted. *Xenophobe's Guide to the English.* London: Oval Books, 2008.

Reuter, Donald F. *Gay-2-Zee: A Dictionary of Sex, Subtext, and the Sublime.* New York: St Martin's Griffin, 2006.

Vallardi, Editore Antonio. *Inglese Slang.* Milan: Antonio Vallardi Editore, 2003.

www.abc.com

www.brainyquotes.com

www.cbs.com

www.cockneyrhymingslang.co.uk

www.coolslang.com

www.imdb.com

www.madonna.com

www.manchestereveningnews.co.uk

www.phrases.org.uk

www.probertencyclopaedia.com

www.scribd.com

www.sex-lexis.com

www.thesexdictionary.com

www.thinkexist.com

www.trendcentral.com

www.urbandictionary.com

www.usnews.com

www.wordreference.com

www.wutang-corp.com

DAILY BENDER

Want Some More?

Hit up our humor blog, The Daily Bender, to get your fill of all things funny—be it subversive, odd, offbeat, or just plain mean. The Bender editors are there to get you through the day and on your way to happy hour. Whether we're linking to the latest video that made us laugh or calling out (or bullshit on) whatever's happening, we've got what you need for a good laugh.

If you like our book, you'll love our blog. (And if you hated it, man up and tell us why.) Visit The Daily Bender for a shot of humor that'll serve you until the bartender can.

VISIT THE DAILY BENDER BLOG TODAY AT
www.adamsmedia.com/blog/humor